M

§ ON POET

ON POETRY

Selected Prose

AND CRAFT

of Theodore Roethke

FOREWORD BY CAROLYN KIZER

 Copper Canyon Press

Foreword by Carolyn Kizer.

Printed in the United States of America.

Copper Canyon acknowledges Gray Foster for the use of her photography on the cover.

Copper Canyon Press thanks Ralph J. Mills, Jr. for the permission to reprint his Introduction to the original edition of *On the Poet and His Craft*.

Copper Canyon Press is in residence under the auspices of the Centrum Foundation at Fort Worden State Park in Port Townsend, Washington. Centrum sponsors artist residencies, education workshops for Washington State students and teachers, blues, jazz, and fiddle tunes festivals, classical music performances, and The Port Townsend Writers' Conference.

LIBRARY OF CONGRESS CATALOGING-IN-PUBLICATION DATA

Roethke, Theodore, 1908–1963
On poetry & craft: selected prose of Theodore Roethke / foreword by Carolyn Kizer.
  p. cm.
ISBN 1-55659-156-x (alk. paper)
1. Roethke, Theodore, 1908–1963 — Authorship. 2. Roethke, Theodore, 1908–1963 — Aesthetics. 3. Poetics. I. Title: On poetry and craft.
II. Kizer, Carolyn. III. Title.
  PS3535.039 A6 2001
808.1 — DC21   2001001017

9 8 7 6 5 4 3 2 FIRST PRINTING

COPPER CANYON PRESS
Post Office Box 271
Port Townsend, Washington 98368
www.coppercanyonpress.org

PUBLISHER'S NOTE

On Poetry & Craft draws upon two previous volumes of
Theodore Roethke's prose, both published posthumously,
On the Poet and His Craft (1965), edited by Ralph J. Mills Jr.,
and *Straw for the Fire: From the Notebooks of Theodore Roethke,
1943–63* (1972), edited by David Wagoner. In compiling this
volume Copper Canyon Press has expanded and relied upon
Mr. Mills's organizational structure — four sections with an
epilogue — but has restructured Part Three to focus on teach-
ing and the classroom. Additionally, the accompanying notes
are adapted from *On the Poet and His Craft*. All sections from
Straw for the Fire were excerpted from Theodore Roethke's
notebooks and were previously compiled and edited by David
Wagoner. Copper Canyon Press would like to thank Mr. Mills
and Mr. Wagoner for their work, and like those two editors,
Copper Canyon Press is grateful for the generous assistance
and encouragement of Beatrice Roethke Lushington.

Contents

ON POETRY & CRAFT

Foreword

BACK IN THE SEVENTIES when I was teaching at Chapel Hill, this outfit in Florida had the brilliant idea of tape recording people who had studied with distinguished poet-teachers. They asked me if I would talk about Roethke, and I said yes. They sent me big reels of tape; they had acquired a studio in Raleigh, and they'd gone to all manner of trouble to set this up; but the more I thought about it the more frozen I got. Time went on and I hadn't done anything; I started getting anxious phone calls from Florida, and finally they said, "Ms. Kizer, are you gonna do this or aren't you?" And I said, "Well, you know, it's too raw; it's too fresh in my mind, his death, and I haven't been able to handle it yet." There was a silence, and the guy at the other end of the phone said, "Do you realize that Theodore Roethke has been dead for thirteen years?" And I said, "No. No, I don't." And this is one of the first times I've really tried to talk about Ted and what his teaching methods were like. I may say that, when I go back and look at my notebooks from those days in his class '55–'56 (and whenever I could get a chance to sit in after that), I'm amazed that my own teaching methods are such a duplicate of his. I'm fascinated by the fact that I really haven't thought up anything much on my own. I've simply carried on as the master taught me.

That first class in '55 was an extraordinary class; in it were James Wright, Jack Gilbert, and a man who's now a distinguished German scholar and head of his university department, named Helmut Bonheim. There was also a seventy-year-old rabbi, a man even older than that who was a retired sea captain who'd just lost his wife and was beside himself with boredom and pain, and people of eighteen. It was the whole spectrum. Ted always insisted on having a class that was open to the public. You didn't have to have any credentials to be in it, you just went and talked to him and he decided whether or not you should be in the class. And so you had a wonderful mix of all kinds of people of all ages, from kids to grandparents.

One of the very striking things about Roethke was his attitude toward these old men in the class. He could be a real brute, particularly when drinking. He was the original male chauvinist pig. But with the rabbi and with the sea captain, he was charmingly deferential because he said that they knew things the rest of us didn't know. They knew what life was like and they had a *subject*. And both these men—the sea captain in particular—contributed a good deal to the class.

When Jim Wright came to class, "we knew at once he was our genius," to quote a poem of mine. Jim came from Kenyon College; he was writing brilliantly, and was well at work on his first book, *St. Judas*. Jack and I were not that far along and I probably doubted if we ever would be. But there was an atmosphere in that classroom that was unlike anything I've ever come across. Whenever I get a chance to have an open class like that I do it, because it is an invaluable experience to have a cross section of people by age and occupation and even by talent. Experience has its own contribution to make, and Ted was always very conscious of that.

The great thing about Ted was that he knew how to make a good poem out of a bad poem. I like to think that he taught me to do this too. I'm not interested in that sort of perfect Iowa Workshop poem, in which everything eccentric or outrageous has been ironed out: one of those neat little poems that is disposable like Kleenex: you read it once (though you may not finish it) and think, "Very nice," and then you never think about it again. But I can take a great, big, messy, ambitious, poem and find its form, and help to shape it up. Ted said many useful things about that kind of poem. One of them was to think of a poem as a three-act play, where you move from one impulse to the next, and then there is a final breath, which is the summation of the action of the whole. He had picked up that wonderful phrase from Sir John Davies which he used in a poem: "She taught me turn, and counter-turn, and stand." Which is the essence of dramatic structure. It's what a long poem has to do. It doesn't require physical action, but there has to be some mental or emotional action that carries through in the poem.

Roethke was an extraordinarily rigorous critic, and if you couldn't take it, you didn't learn much. For example, he said the real test was that every line of a poem should be a poem. That's about as tough as you can get. I apply that to my own work and sometimes just throw up my hands. But I find it's extremely useful in getting rid of connectives, passive constructions, surplus adjectives, and words that don't have any particular energy in them.

He was a fanatic about active verbs. He used to give us lists of verbs from seventeenth-century poets, particularly Vaughn, and say, "How many of these can you incorporate in a poem?" He intensely disliked participles. I remember that one time, as I was sedulously following him, I made my speech to a class about passive constructions and a smart student said, "What about 'To be or not to be'?" I said, "Well, that explains Hamlet's nature: his ambivalence, his uncertainty—his basic passivity," and I got out of that one! In another class somebody said, "What about 'Turning and turning in the widening gyre'?" (I've had some smart—and smart-ass— students!) I replied, "When you can write as well as Yeats, you won't need to be in this class." But in general those are good practices.

Another thing Ted used to do which I often do with students was tell them, "Take out all the adjectives and see what you've got left. See which ones are absolutely essential to the poem." It's amazing how poems are improved. Sometimes when they're pared down like that, they speak wonderfully to you. This again was part of his obsession and fascination with the seventeenth century. People like Herbert and Donne and Vaughn use very few adjectives. The whole strength of the poem rests on the verb. The verb is the great armature around which the language of the poem is wrapped, as I've said many times.

Sometimes Roethke would say sort of arbitrarily, "Cut a line out of each stanza," if he felt the poem was a little flaccid, a little loose. So you'd have to conflate two or three lines to make this work. Most times even when we didn't think it would work, it did. Ted would also ruthlessly cut stanzas that he thought were not on the main track of the poem. The first poem I had that was widely anthologized was a poem about the death of my mother called "The Great Blue Heron." Ted took two stanzas out of it. It was because

I trusted him so much that I agreed to do this although I felt like an amputee. Within two months I couldn't even remember what was missing. He pointed out something to me that I have noticed all my life since, and that is when you take out a big hunk of a poem, the part that comes before and the part that comes after the cut just seal up, including the rhymes, as if you had discovered the poem's true form, the form the poem had been trying to make you understand all the time.

Roethke was very concerned with trying other forms when a poem wasn't working particularly well. He'd say, "Put it in triplets, try it in couplets," and "The thing about these shorter stanzas is they leave a lot of white space, and you can see if those lines will stand up by themselves." When you write a long, dense poem and you haven't bothered to make stanzas or you've got long shapeless stanzas, you can get away with a lot. Whitman got away with a lot. Ginsberg does. In a forest of verbiage, you see clearly to deploy enough intellectual rigor to the lines.

Another thing he said that was just as difficult as saying that every line of a poem should be a poem was to say, "Read down the first words in each line and see if they make a kind of poem; if they're nothing but 'and,' 'but,' 'so,' 'thus,' 'maybe,' then try to make the first word of each line interesting." I could open a book almost at random and take the first word of each line: "on," "king-dom," "fetter," "worst," "saliva," "agony," "lust," "how," "dreams," "bleak," "great," "not." See how close that is to being a poem?

Other pieces of his good advice: "If you find you have great facility in something, work against it." He noticed that I rhymed with ease, so he warned me against too many perfect rhymes, and too many end-rhymes. "Bury them in the line!" he said. And I've done that. One must always try to do what one can't do, and not what one can do already.

When it came to editing the poem, Ted would say, "Any fool can cut a bad line. It takes a real pro to cut a good line." But how we cling to those good lines that are just salad-dressing, irrelevant, or that don't advance the movement of the poem! So we play a little game when we cut out the goodies; we tell ourselves that we'll put them in another poem. Sometimes these lines are the impetus for another poem, like starter for sourdough. But usually they just keep traveling from poem to poem. You can cannibalize a car far more easily than you can a poem.

But the most important thing Roethke ever said to me was after class when another student was very critical of some eccentric thing I had done, and Ted admonished him, "You want to be very careful when you criticize something like that, because it may be the hallmark of an emerging style." He knew that our eccentricities are part of our true voice.

And he was a great deal more disciplined than he is given credit for by people who didn't know him. I believe he wrote every day— wrote and read and made notes in an ever increasing pile of notebooks. It was from these voluminous notebooks that David Wagoner assembled *Straws for the Fire*. Ted would put down a little phrase here and a little phrase there, and brood about them. One of the reasons he sometimes plagiarized was that he didn't always take note of who had said what.

Although, as I've said, Ted was this ferocious male chauvinist in private life, in class he was somebody else. The people he loved to quote from were women poets. Louise Bogan. Leonie Adams. The obscure English poet Ruth Pitter, who died at the age of ninety-five. I can still hear Ted reciting her poem:

> But for lust we could be friends.
>> On each others' necks, could weep:
> In each others' arms could sleep
>> In the calm the cradle lends:
>
> Lends awhile and takes away.
>> But for hunger, but for fear,
> Calm could be our day and year
>> From the yellow to the grey:
>
> From the gold to the grey hair...

I know it all by heart. Ted was very big on memorization. "There will be times in your life," he used to say in his growly voice, "when you will be trapped. You won't have anything to read, you'll be in the line at the supermarket, you'll be sitting in the dentist's office, and if you've got those poems in your head, it's not just that they will help you with your work, they will help you through the dry times in your life." And they do. But it's hard to get students to memorize poems. Most of them are very resistant.

I think Bogan's tracks are quite easy to follow in Ted's early poems. For example, "Thought does not crush to stone. / The great sledge drops in vain. / Truth never is undone; / Its shafts remain." That's just Bogan all over the place. And so in a way is "My secrets cry aloud. / I have no need for tongue," the first poem in *Open House*. They had a wonderful exchange of advice about their poems. They taught each other a great deal, and she ended up being his "best woman" when he got married to Beatrice O'Connell. The people who stood up with him were Louise Bogan and W.H. Auden; that's pretty grand.

One of the things that he talked a lot about with Louise was the way she began poems with a prepositional phrase: "Beyond the hour we counted rain that fell...," "Under thunder dark, the cicadas resound...," "Over our head, if we but know...." There are at least a dozen poems, some of Louise's very best poems, that begin with a prepositional phrase. What's the virtue of that? You're plunged into the middle of the poem. There's no winding up. There's no setting of the stage, no description of fields, and trees, and poppies, and emotional states, and so on. You're right there.

Leonie Adams is one of the most neglected modern figures, partly because she's a pure lyric poet, partly because she's not only lyric, she's metaphysical and she's difficult. And I would like to see Leonie brought back into prominence at some point, because she was a lovely poet and a lovely human being.

Now when I read John Clare's poem "The Badger," I can hear Roethke's voice reading it. He had this rather deep, growly voice, and this poem is full of wonderful plosives, powerful monosyllables, and they relentlessly pound away at you. Technically it's an extraordinary poem, and Ted relished every beat of it. But I think other than Kunitz, Yeats, and Clare, I can't remember other male poets that he used to quote in class, oddly enough. He certainly never quoted any of his contemporaries, other than Kunitz, who was then largely unknown, although fiftyish. Lowell and Jarrell were very much presences. I think there was an element of competition there, but Ted felt very strongly that you need to learn from your seniors rather than your contemporaries. I remember him saying something to the effect that you would be too influenced by the mannerisms of the poets which might be exactly the things that made them fade from view. He liked to go back to the seventeenth century, as Clare did. He skipped happily over the nineteenth century, and most of the eighteenth, to where the English language was fresh and precise.

One of Ted's greatest attributes as a teacher is that none of us who studied with him write at all like Roethke. If Ted caught any of us imitating him we never did it again. He would tease us mercilessly. Hugo and Wagoner were students of Ted before our group, and after us came Sandra McPherson and Tess Gallagher. I can always spot a Hugo student. I was in Buffalo, I think, and a girl showed me a poem in class and I said, "When did you study with Richard Hugo?" and she was absolutely floored. "How did you know?" Dick had a set of rules, which I've been trying for years to get a copy of, that guaranteed that you would write a Richard Hugo poem. We always made excuses for Hugo: he was insecure, and was comforted by followers. Well, Ted was insecure too, but he didn't do that.

Bill Matthews has said that a really good writing teacher wants you to write more and more like yourself, while a less good teacher wants you to write like him or her—only slightly less well! It's almost guaranteed that if you're imitating somebody else, it will be less good—which is not to say that you shouldn't experiment by imitating others, but that these experiments should be confined to your notebook.

Several poets whom I admire are somewhat crazy; and they contain that nuttiness by the use of sophisticated form. I confess to a deep weakness for the poetry of Bill Knott, for example. Of course Roethke really was crazy, in the clinical sense, so poetry was a life and death matter for him. He was a manic-depressive (misdiagnosed for years as a schizophrenic), and at the high end of the spectrum he wrote bad poetry, and in the low end he couldn't write at all, so he had to catch the muse in the periods in between. A lot of nonsense has been written about Ted as crazy all the time or drunk all the time. I picked up an English literary magazine the other day—the English always get us wrong, you know—where someone said that Roethke wrote some of his best poems when he was drunk. Nobody writes a good poem when drunk, with the possible exception of Patrick Kavanaugh!

I saw Ted drink a lot, but rarely drunk. His guests were more often drunk than he. I remember parties in his garden in the summer, in Seattle: very hot and humid. Ted would be wandering around with a large martini pitcher, topping off your drink at frequent intervals, and because you had lost count of how much you had consumed, you had drunk seven martinis, and were reeling.

Two great events in Ted's life after I got to know him—aside from the major breakdowns—were, first, the death of Dylan Thomas. This was a great shock to him, and which caused him to think long, long thoughts about reforming. As a result, he seriously tried to cut down on his drinking and roistering, and committed himself firmly to heterosexuality. (How seriously his erotic forays in this department were can only be speculated upon; I suspect it was mainly boastful talk.) The second great thing was when he met and married Beatrice O'Connell, which further stabilized his life and which resulted in the greatest love poems since Yeats. Beatrice was a great beauty: so decorative, so quiet, such a great cook! What every man wants! Then there was this outpouring of magnificent poems:

"I knew a woman, lovely in her bones…" and those "memorable lines" ("Quote me a memorable line," I've heard Ted say dozens of times) from "Words for the Wind":

> Passion's enough to give
> Shape to a random joy:
> I cry delight: I know
> The root, the core of a cry.
> Swan-heart, arbutus-calm,
> She moves when time is shy:
> Love has a thing to do
>
> Under the rising moon;
> I smile, no mineral man;

> I bear, but not alone,
> The burden of this joy.

A whole series of ravishing poems that one cannot read or reread without tears. But as Ted grew older, between bouts of mental illness that occurred increasingly often, he began to think more and more about death, so much so that his death was a shock but not a surprise. But these meditations led to poems like "In a Dark Time," one of the great poems in the language.

Some people have a difficult time with the poems of his middle period that use what Roethke called "pre-verbal" material, or the nursery rhyme cadences that occur in "The Lost Son" and other poems of that period. Rereading the poem I'm struck by how heavily spondaic it is, spondee after spondee: Listen to them: "dead cry," "slow drip," "soft-sigh," "hard time," "old wound," "one fly"—all these in the first nineteen lines. I used to have a theory—I may still —that you could tell a natural-born poet from the outset by the instinctive use of spondees.

Throughout the poem the poet asks questions, a very effective device. It brings the reader right into the poem, a participant: "Tell me / Which is the way I take: / Out of what door do I go, / Where and to whom?" Then he makes frequent use of the pathetic fallacy, not just to try to animate forms in nature, but to reveal mental unease, a man talking to a tree. Then he moves into nursery rhyme or skip-rope rhyme cadences:

> The shape of a rat?
> It's bigger than that.
> It's less than a leg
> And more than a nose,
> Just under the water
> It usually goes.

I'll say more about these cadences in a minute, but first I want to mark the entrance of James Joyce. You will find echoes of or parallels with *Portrait of the Artist as a Young Man* throughout: the image of the rat under the water, symbol of adolescent sexual anxiety. The passage in Part 3: "From the mouths of jugs / Perched on many shelves, / I saw substance flowing / That cold morning": right out of *Portrait*! Whether consciously or not, who can say? How little we know about the common experiences of sensitive alienated children!

To get back to the jump-rope rhymes: Ted admitted freely that he was influenced by Iona and Peter Opie, husband and wife, who hung around children's playgrounds in England and listened to their games. They often proved that many of these rhyming games go way back in time: jokes about, say, King Charles and his mistress are handed down and updated to jokes about the Prince of Wales, the earlier one, and Mrs. Simpson. (I suppose now there are jokes about the present Prince of Wales and his Camilla.) None of this material had been written down until the Opies came along. A pure example of the last remaining vestiges of the oral tradition—from Homer to hop-scotch! Ted was fascinated by the oral tradition, and used its mnemonic devices for what may be the first time in modern poetry. Other poets have since become concerned with what you might call Ur-poetry. As Bill Matthews has said, reading it is like getting to know diamonds when they were still leaves.

But I'd like to speak a bit about the over all structure of the poem. It's useful to regard it as if it were a Noh play. In the Noh, the principal characters are ghosts, and the action of the play is a flashback. They are in limbo, and are trying to ascend to a higher state of consciousness by achieving self-knowledge. They acquire understanding by reliving the past. This is what Roethke is doing, in symbolic language, until he gets to Part 4, "The Return," which is straight autobiography. That tyrannical old German, Otto Roethke, makes his appearance with the words "Pipe-knock," standing on a single line. Then, "Scurry of warm over small plants. / Ordnung! ordnung! / Papa is coming!" "Pipe-knock" of course is a wonderful double: the father is knocking his pipe against a pipe which heats the famous Roethke greenhouse. And the pipe itself knocks!

There is another way of looking at the poem: Stanley Kunitz once said that the shape of any poem can be described in symbols: a circle, two sides of a triangle, up-side and down-side, and so on. A striking example of a down-side or avalanche shape is Hopkins' "The Leaden Echo and the Golden Echo," where the poem goes down to the basement of the soul with the lines. "Be beginning to despair, to despair / Despair, despair, despair, despair." Then, with the single word, "Spare!" alone on the next line, the poem begins its ascent. Ted surely learned from this as both poets learned from Dante.

Roethke's poem shows the flight of the madman down into the depths. Part 2 is called "The Pit." Part 3 is "The Gibber": Nature is against him, the weeds, the snakes, the cows and briars tell him, "Die." The line "Look, look, the ditch is running white" is a final echo of Joyce; like the water in the jug overflowing, a masturbatory image. Then comes Part 4, "The Return" where the poem begins its ascent, structurally very similar to Hopkins, and ends with "It was beginning winter," where the poem achieves increasing sanity and calm: "The weeds stopped swinging. / The mind moved, not alone, / Through the clear air, in the silence." An exhausted kind of peace, but questioning still. The poem takes on a metaphysical resonance at the end—Eliotic if you will—where the poet asks a series of short questions; and then come the final lines: "A lively understandable spirit / once entertained you. / It will come again. / Be still. / Wait." And the poet awaits a spiritual re-birth. Let's leave Ted there: expectant, and tranquil, as I hope his spirit is.

Carolyn Kizer

Part One

Some Self-Analysis

This student essay was one of a number Roethke
wrote at the University of Michigan and was proba-
bly composed during his sophomore year, 1926–27.

I EXPECT THIS COURSE to open my eyes to story material, to un-
leash my too dormant imagination, to develop that quality utterly
lacking in my nature—a sense of form. I do not expect to acquire
much technique. I expect to be able to seize upon the significant,
reject the trivial. I hope to acquire a greater love for humanity in all
its forms.

I have long wondered just what my strength was as a writer. I am
often filled with tremendous enthusiasm for a subject, yet my writ-
ing about it will seem a sorry attempt. Above all, I possess a driving
sincerity,—that prime virtue of any creative worker. I write only
what I believe to be the absolute truth,—even if I must ruin the
theme in so doing. In this respect I feel far superior to those glib
people in my classes who often garner better grades than I do.
They are so often pitiful frauds,—artificial—insincere. They have
a line that works. They do not write from the depths of their hearts.
Nothing of theirs was ever born of pain. Many an incoherent yet
sincere piece of writing has outlived the polished product.

I write only about people and things that I know thoroughly.
Perhaps I have become a mere reporter, not a writer. Yet I feel that
this is all my present abilities permit. I will open my eyes in my
youth and store this raw, living material. Age may bring the fire that
molds experience into artistry.

I have a genuine love of nature. It is not the least bit affected, but
an integral and powerful part of my life. I know that Cooper is a
fraud—that he doesn't give a true sense of the sublimity of American

scenery. I know that Muir and Thoreau and Burroughs speak the truth.

I can sense the moods of nature almost instinctively. Ever since I could walk, I have spent as much time as I could in the open. A perception of nature—no matter how delicate, how subtle, how evanescent,—remains with me forever.

I am influenced too much, perhaps, by natural objects. I seem bound by the very room I'm in. I've associated so long with prosaic people that I've dwarfed myself spiritually. When I get alone under an open sky where man isn't too evident,—then I'm tremendously exalted and a thousand vivid ideas and sweet visions flood my consciousness.

I think that I possess story material in abundance. I have had an unusual upbringing. I was let alone, thank God! My mother insisted upon two things,—that I strive for perfection in whatever I did and that I always try to be a gentleman. I played with Italians, with Russians, Poles, and the "sissies" on Michigan avenue. I was carefully watched, yet allowed to follow my own inclinations. I have seen a good deal of life that would never have been revealed to an older person. Up to the time I came to college then I had seen humanity in diverse forms. Now I'm cramped and unhappy. I don't feel that these idiotic adolescents are worth writing about. In the summer, I turn animal and work for a few weeks in a factory. Then I'm happy.

My literary achievements have been insignificant. At fourteen, I made a speech which was translated into twenty-six languages and used as Red Cross propaganda. When I was younger, it seemed that everything I wrote was eminently successful. I always won a prize when I entered an essay contest. In college, I've been able to get only one "A" in four rhetoric courses. I feel this keenly. If I can't write, what can I do? I wonder.

When I was a freshman, I told Carlton Wells that I knew I could write whether he thought so or not. On my next theme he wrote "You can Write!" How I have cherished that praise!

It is bad form to talk about grades, I know. If I don't get an "A" in this course, it wouldn't be because I haven't tried. I've made a slow start. I'm going to spend Christmas vacation writing. A "B" symbolizes defeat to me. I've been beaten too often.

I do wish that we were allowed to keep our stories until we felt that we had worked them into the best possible form.

I do not have the divine urge to write. There seems to be something surging within,—a profound undercurrent of emotion. Yet there is none of that fertility of creation which distinguishes the real writer.

Nevertheless, I have faith in myself. I'm either going to be a good writer or a poor fool.

An American Poet Introduces Himself and His Poems

Presented as a BBC broadcast, July 30, 1953
(Disc #SLO 34254).

EVERYONE KNOWS THAT AMERICA is a continent, but few Europeans realize the various and diverse parts of this land. The Saginaw Valley, where I was born, had been great lumbering country in the 1880s. It is very fertile flat country in Michigan, and the principal towns, Saginaw and Flint, lie at the northern edge of what is now the central industrial area of the United States.

It was to this region that my grandfather came in from Prussia, where he had been Bismarck's head forester. He and his sons started some greenhouses which became the most extensive in that part of America.

It was a wonderful place for a child to grow up in and around. There were not only twenty-five acres in the town, mostly under glass and intensely cultivated, but farther out in the country the last stand of virgin timber in the Saginaw Valley and, elsewhere, a wild area of cutover second-growth timber, which my father and uncle made into a small game preserve.

As a child, then, I had several worlds to live in, which I felt were mine. One favorite place was a swampy corner of the game sanctuary where herons always nested. I put down one of my earlier memories in a poem about them:

> The heron stands in water where the swamp
> Has deepened to the blackness of a pool,
> Or balances with one leg on a hump
> Of marsh grass heaped above a musk-rat hole.

He walks the shallow with an antic grace.
The great feet break the ridges of the sand,
The long eye notes the minnow's hiding place.
His beak is quicker than a human hand.

He jerks a frog across his bony lip,
Then points his heavy bill above the wood.
The wide wings flap but once to lift him up.
A single ripple starts from where he stood.

What the greenhouses themselves were to me I try to indicate in my second book, *The Lost Son and Other Poems*, published in this country [England] in 1949. They were to me, I realize now, both heaven and hell, a kind of tropics created in the savage climate of Michigan, where austere German Americans turned their love of order and their terrifying efficiency into something truly beautiful. It was a universe, several worlds, which, even as a child, one worried about, and struggled to keep alive, as in the poem "Big Wind":

Where were the greenhouses going,
Lunging into the lashing
Wind driving water
So far down the river
All the faucets stopped? —
So we drained the manure-machine
For the steam plant,
Pumping the stale mixture
Into the rusty boilers,
Watching the pressure gauge
Waver over to red,
As the seams hissed
And the live steam
Drove to the far
End of the rose-house,
Where the worst wind was,
Creaking the cypress window-frames,
Cracking so much thin glass
We stayed all night,
Stuffing the holes with burlap;
But she rode it out,
That old rose-house,
She hove into the teeth of it,
The core and pith of that ugly storm,

Ploughing with her stiff prow,
Bucking into the wind-waves
That broke over the whole of her,
Flailing her sides with spray,
Flinging long strings of wet across the roof-top,
Finally veering, wearing themselves out, merely
Whistling thinly under the wind-vents;
She sailed until the calm morning,
Carrying her full cargo of roses.

In those first poems I had begun, like the child, with small things and had tried to make plain words do the trick. Somewhat later, in 1945, I began a series of longer pieces which try, in their rhythms, to catch the movement of the mind itself, to trace the spiritual history of a protagonist (not "I" personally but of all haunted and harried men); to make this sequence a true and not arbitrary order which would permit many ranges of feeling, including humor.

All these states of mind were to be rendered dramatically, without comment, without allusion, the action often implied or indicated in the interior monologue or dialogue between the self and its mentor, or conscience, or, sometimes, another person.

How to create a reality, a verisimilitude, the "as if" of the child's world, in language a child would use, was, for me, enormously difficult. For instance, the second poem, "I Need, I Need," opens with very oral imagery, the child's world of sucking and licking. Then there is a shift to a passage in which two children are jumping rope. The reader isn't *told* the children are jumping rope: he simply hears the two reciting, alternately, jingles to each other; then this mingled longing and aggressiveness changes, in the next passage, to a vaguely felt, but definite, feeling of love in one of the children:

1.

A deep dish. Lumps in it.
I can't taste my mother.
Hoo. I know the spoon.
Sit in my mouth.

A sneeze can't sleep.
Diddle we care
Couldly.

Went down cellar,
Talked to a faucet;
The drippy water
Had nothing to say.

Whisper me over,
Why don't you, begonia,
There's no alas
Where I live.

Scratched the wind with a stick.
The leaves liked it.
Do the dead bite?
Mamma, she's a sad fat.

A dove said dove all day.
A hat is a house.
I hid in his.

...

3.
Stop the larks. Can I have my heart back?
Today I saw a beard in a cloud.
The ground cried my name:
Good-bye for being wrong.
Love helps the sun.
But not enough.

4.
When you plant, spit in the pot.
A pick likes to hit ice.
Hooray for me and mice! —
The oats are all right.

Hear me, soft ears and roundy stones!
It's a dear life I can touch.
Who's ready for pink and frisk?
My hoe eats like a goat.

Her feet said yes.
It was all hay.
I said to the gate,
Who else knows

> What water does?
> Dew ate the fire.

> I know another fire.
> Has roots.

In the subsequent poems we hear the young adolescent, half a child, then the randy young man boasting and caterwauling; and finally more difficult passages in which the mind, under great stress, roves far back into the subconscious, later emerging into the "light" of more serene or euphoric passages at the end of each phase of experience.

Sometimes, of course, there is a regression. I believe that the spiritual man must go back in order to go forward. The way is circuitous, and sometimes lost, but invariably returned to.

Some of the technical skills characteristic of this sequence — the rapidly shifting metaphor, the rhetorical questions, and the like — reappear in more formal poems completed recently, entitled "Four for Sir John Davies," which are, among other things, a tribute to the Elizabethan author of "Orchestra" and to the late W.B. Yeats.

THE DANCE

> Is that dance slowing in the mind of man
> That made him think the universe could hum?
> The great wheel turns its axle when it can;
> I need a place to sing, and dancing-room,
> And I have made a promise to my ears
> I'll sing and whistle romping with the bears.

> For they are all my friends: I saw one slide
> Down a steep hillside on a cake of ice, —
> Or was that in a book? I think with pride:
> A caged bear rarely does the same thing twice
> In the same way: O watch his body sway! —
> This animal remembering to be gay.

> I tried to fling my shadow at the moon,
> The while my blood leaped with a wordless song.
> Though dancing needs a master, I had none

To teach my toes to listen to my tongue.
But what I learned there, dancing all alone,
Was not the joyless motion of a stone.

I take this cadence from a man named Yeats;
I take it, and I give it back again:
For other tunes and other wanton beats
Have tossed my heart and fiddled through my brain.
Yes, I was dancing-mad, and how
That came to be the bears and Yeats would know.

Theodore Roethke

From *Twentieth Century Authors, First Supplement*, edited by Stanley J. Kunitz (New York: H.W. Wilson, 1955).

I MIGHT MANAGE TO WRITE an anecdotal and perhaps even semi-engaging and mildly witty account of my life; but of what importance is it that I grew up in and around a beautiful greenhouse owned by my father and uncle; that I hated high school and Michigan and Harvard (in spite of fine teachers like Strauss, Campbell, Rice, I.A. Richards, and others); that I have taught in various colleges and coached tennis; worked in a pickle factory for several seasons; have lived, alternately, very quietly and then foolishly and violently; that I have been called "as good a steak cook as Brancusi" by William Carlos Williams; and that the kids at Bennington in a burst of misdirected generosity called me "the best teacher we ever had"; that my books have been treated with astonishing generosity by good critics and poets and the young; that the English seem to like me even better; and that I mean almost nothing (except for a handful of personal friends) to the people of my own state, to the man in the street—and desire that regard most passionately; that I am much interested in oral presentation.

All such details, and others like them, seem particularly trivial and vulgar in my case because I have tried to put them down in poems, as barely and honestly as possible, symbolically, what few nuggets of observation and, let us hope, spiritual wisdom I have managed to seize upon in the course of a conventional albeit sometimes disordered existence. I have tried to transmute and purify my "life," the sense of being defiled by it, in both small and formal and somewhat blunt short poems, and latterly, in longer poems which try in their rhythms to catch the very movement of the mind itself, to trace the spiritual history of a protagonist (not "I," personally), of all haunted and harried men; to make in this series (now probably finished) a true and not arbitrary order which will permit many ranges of feeling, including humor.

I began, like the child, with small things. I had no interest in verse after an intense period of pleasure in nursery rhymes in English and German and songs my mother and my nurse sang me. I really wanted, at fifteen and sixteen, to write a beautiful, a "chiseled" prose as it was called in those days. There were books at home and I went to the local libraries (and very good ones they were for such a smallish town); read Stevenson, Pater, Newman, Tomlinson, and those maundering English charm boys known as familiar essayists. I bought on my own editions of Emerson, Thoreau, and, as God's my witness, subscribed to the *Dial* when I was in the seventh grade. I was strong for anthologies of great thoughts, including Elbert Hubbard; and had such deep interest in the short story that I started buying the O'Brien anthologies in 1920 when I was twelve. (You could make money in the short story!)

My first verses, and dreadful they were, I sold for $1. About a year later when I was moping through the Harvard Yard one night, I saw a man I thought might be Robert Hillyer. I said boldly, "Pardon me, Sir, I think I have some poems you might like." A look of pain came over his face. "Come to my office at eleven," he said. I did, complete with fur coat and a fancy suit (those Harvards weren't going to have it over me!). Ushered in by his secretary he took the verse, started reading. Suddenly he wheeled in his chair. "Any editor who wouldn't buy this is a fool!" he said. I was overwhelmed (though I had thought so too!). There were only three poems, but Ridgely Torrence of the *New Republic* and George Shuster, then of *Commonweal*, did buy two of them.

I felt I had come to the end (really the beginning) of a trail. I had learned how to get high grades, but that seemed meaningless. Now I didn't have to go into advertising (I had written at eighteen copy which had been used in national campaigns), or the law. I wasn't just a spoiled sad snob. I could write and people I respected printed the stuff.

It took me ten years to complete one little book, and now some of the things in it seem to creak. Still, I like about ten pieces in it. Writers were extraordinarily generous to me in a very personal way in this long incubation, particularly in what not to do. Let me name some: W.H. Auden, Louise Bogan, Malcolm Cowley, Babette Deutsch, Rolfe Humphries, John Holmes, Stanley Kunitz, Douglas Moore, A.J.M. Smith, William Carlos Williams, and latterly, Kenneth Burke, Edith Sitwell, and many students. These people, maybe without realizing it, spoke with absolute candor and often with great insight; they often kept me from going down blind alleys or wasting what time I had for writing better.

I write this down because it is a matter rarely mentioned. I owe much less, I believe, to the *work* of contemporaries than to their qualities as men and women. And that debt is immense.

Theodore Roethke Writes...

Appeared originally in the *Poetry Book Society*
Bulletin (London), No. 16, December 1957.

IT IS AN ESPECIAL PLEASURE for an American to thank the Poetry
Book Society for making *Words for the Wind* its Christmas choice.

The volume really consists of two books: earlier work and later.
Since it is his last things which most interest a poet, let me dwell on
these briefly.

I believe a book should reveal as many sides of a writer as is de-
cent for him to show: that these aspects be brought together in
some kind of coherent whole that is recognizable to the careful
reader. This means that some poems will sometimes support other
poems, either by being complements to them, or by providing con-
trasts. Thus, the first section of love poems in *Words for the Wind*
contains pieces tender or highly romantic, others are "witty,"
coarse, and sensual. It is my hope that a reader will like both kinds
of thing. Then by way of contrast, there is a handful of light pieces
and poems for children. These are rougher than what most chil-
dren's editors prefer. The attempt—part of a larger effort—was to
make poems which please both child and parent, without insulting
the intelligence or taste of either.

The third section of these later pieces consists of poems of terror,
and running away—and the dissociation of personality that occurs
in such attempts to escape reality. In these the protagonist is alive
in space, almost against his will; his world is the cold and dark
known to subhuman things.

There follows a series of poems dedicated to W.B. Yeats.
Highly formal stylistically, these poems are related to the sixteenth
century, with lines severely end-stopped, for the most part.

Finally comes a sequence of longish poems "Meditations of an

Old Woman." The protagonist is modeled, in part, after my own mother, now dead, whose favorite reading was the Bible, Jane Austen, and Dostoyevsky—in other words, a gentle, highly articulate old lady believing in the glories of the world, yet fully conscious of its evils. These poems use a technique of developing themes alternately, a method employed in "Praise to the End!," an earlier sequence, a kind of old spiritual autobiography beginning with the very small child. Of these last poems I have said:[1]

> ... Much of the action is implied or, particularly in the case of erotic experience, rendered obliquely. The revelation of the identity of the speaker may itself be a part of the drama; or, in some instances, in a dream sequence, his identity may merge with someone else's, or be deliberately blurred. This struggle for spiritual identity is, of course, one of the perpetual recurrences. (This is not the same as the fight of the adolescent personality for recognition in the "real" world.) Disassociation often precedes a new state of clarity.
>
> Rhythmically, it's the spring and rush of the child I'm after —and Gammer Gurton's concision: *mutterkin's* wisdom. Most of the time the material seems to demand a varied short line. I believe that, in this kind of poem, the poet, in order to be true to what is most universal in himself, should not rely on allusion; should not comment or employ many judgment words; should not meditate (or maunder). He must scorn being "mysterious" or loosely oracular, but be willing to face up to genuine mystery. His language must be compelling and immediate: he must create an actuality. He must be able to telescope image and symbol, if necessary, without relying on the obvious connectives: to speak in a kind of psychic shorthand when his protagonist is under great stress. He must be able to shift his rhythms rapidly, the "tension." He works intuitively, and the final form of his poem must be imaginatively right. If intensity has compressed the language so it seems, on early reading, obscure, this obscurity should break open suddenly for the serious reader who can hear the language: the "meaning" itself should come as a dramatic revelation, an excitement. The clues will be scattered richly—as life scatters them; the symbols will mean what they usually mean—and sometimes something more.

---

1. In "Open Letter," from *Mid-Century American Poets*, edited by John Ciardi. The full text of "Open Letter" is given in the present collection.

Words for the Wind opens with some very plain little bits of verse and descriptive pieces about a greenhouse I grew up in and around.

But it is the longish pieces that really break the ground—if any ground is broken. And it is these that I hope the younger readers, in particular, will come to cherish.

I think of myself as a poet of love, a poet of praise. And I wish to be read aloud.

On "Identity"

A statement made at a Northwestern University panel on "Identity" in February 1963.

I REMEMBER THE LATE E.E. Cummings once answered a questionnaire — from *New Verse*, the English magazine of the thirties: answered it by quotations from his own work. At the time, being a fierce, youngish man, I thought this a bit exhibitionistic: but now I'm beginning to see the point. One has said a thing as best one can in the poem — in usually a dramatic context: why debase it or water it down to a didactic prose for a lazy modern audience. But this is not a lazy audience, but a young, idealistic, and deeply serious audience: I can judge by its letters, its questions, indeed, I have been astonished at the pertinence, the relevance of the general subjects; and even more astonished by the fact that, I judge from Mr. Payson Wilde's letter, all this has official credence and sanction. It would seem you have administrators who read — even books.

I take it that we are faced with at least four principal themes: (1) The multiplicity, the chaos of modern life; (2) The way, the means of establishing a personal identity, a self in the face of that chaos; (3) The nature of creation, that faculty for producing order out of disorder in the arts, particularly in poetry; and (4) The nature of God Himself.

I take it as the poet, the intuitive man, I am entitled to, am expected to, throw out what suggestions, what hints I can from my own work, from my own life. I think of this life as an instrument, as an example; and I am perfectly willing to appear ridiculous, absurd, if a real point can be established, a real dent can be made.

I had reason to be delighted with Mr. Bracken's letter: after all he quoted from my work four times. An all-time record. "Nice young man," I thought; "either going to go far, or go entirely mad."

Besides, his prose was better than mine. I felt that, in Kierkegaar-
dian terms, we had reached the true state of education in one
bound: the student was teaching the teacher. Behind his letter and
the various statements I received, one could sense a real hunger for
a reality more than the immediate: a desire not only for a finality,
for a consciousness beyond the mundane but a desire for quietude,
a desire for joy. Now this desire is what the drunkard, the saint, the
mystic hankers for in varying ways:—a purity, a final innocence—
the phrase is Mr. Spender's. I think we Americans are very wistful
about it. Yet we continue to make a fetish of "thing-hood," we sur-
round ourselves with junk, ugly objects endlessly repeated in an
economy dedicated to waste. Hence the possible relevance of my
quotation from "Dolor," which I repeat in part:

> I have known the inexorable sadness of pencils,
> Neat in their boxes, dolor of pad and paper-weight,
> …
> And I have seen dust from the walls of institutions,
> Finer than flour, alive, more dangerous than silica,
> Sift, almost invisible, through long afternoons of tedium,
> Dropping a fine film of nails and delicate eyebrows,
> Glazing the pale hair, the duplicate gray standard faces.

This poem is an exposition of one of the modern hells: the institu-
tion that overwhelms the individual man. The "order," the trivia of
the institution, is, in human terms, a disorder, and as such, must be
resisted. It's truly a sign of psychic health that the young are already
aware of this. How far-reaching all this is, how subtle its ramifica-
tions, how disastrous to the human psyche—to worship bigness,
the firm, the university; numbers, even, let me say, the organized
team effort.

The human problem is to find out what one really *is:* whether
one exists, whether existence is possible. But how? "Am I but noth-
ing, leaning toward a thing?" I think of what I wrote and felt nearly
thirty years ago in a period of ill-health and economic terror—the
first poem in my first book. The middle stanza says:

> My truths are all foreknown,
> This anguish self-revealed.

I'm naked to the bone,
With nakedness my shield.
Myself is what I wear:
I keep the spirit spare.

The last stanza was personally prophetic:

The anger will endure,
The deed will speak the truth
In language strict and pure.
I stop the lying mouth:
Rage warps my clearest cry
To witless agony.

All this has been said before, in Thoreau, in Rilke.

I was going through, though I didn't realize it at the time, a stage that all contemplative men must go through. This poem is a clumsy, innocent, desperate asseveration. I am not speaking of the empirical self, the flesh-bound ego; it's a single word: *myself*, the aggregate of the several selves, if you will. The spirit or soul — should we say the self, once perceived, *becomes* the soul? — this I was keeping "spare" in my desire for the essential. But the spirit need not be spare: it can grow gracefully and beautifully like a tendril, like a flower. I did not know this at the time. This sense I tried later to describe, metaphorically, many times:

The spirit moves,
Yet stays:
Stirs as a blossom stirs,
Still wet from its bud-sheath,
Slowly unfolding,
Turning in the light with its tendrils;
Plays as a minnow plays,
Tethered to a limp weed, swinging,
Tail around, nosing in and out of the current,
Its shadows loose, a watery finger;
Moves, like the snail,
Still inward,
Taking and embracing its surroundings,
Never wishing itself away,
Unafraid of what it is,

A music in a hood,
A small thing,
Singing.

Nor need this final self, or spirit, be a foulness, a disgusting thing from which we should be delivered. A stanza from Stanley Kunitz says:

Father, the darkness of the self goes out
And spreads contagion on the flowing air.
I walk obscurely in a cloud of dark:
Yea, when I kneeled, the dark kneeled down with me.
Touch me: my folds and my defenses fall;
I stand within myself, myself my shield.

This is far more complex than my little stanza, with a great line: "Yea, when I kneeled, the dark kneeled down with me." But this sense of contamination, the "my taste was me," is *not* a necessity: we need *not* be guilt-ridden—if we are pure in heart. It may, of course, as in the Kunitz stanza, be a prelude to a real psychic purgation.

But the young often do have an acute sense of defilement, a hatred of the body. Thus I remember marking this feeling in a violent little poem:

I hate my epidermal dress,
The savage blood's obscenity,
The rags of my anatomy,
And willingly would I dispense
With false accouterments of sense,
To sleep immodestly, a most
Incarnadine and carnal ghost.

Hyperbole, of course, but behind it is still the same desire for a reality of the spirit. Again I was wrong. For the body should be cherished: a temple of God, some Christians say.[2]

In any quest for identity today—or any day—we run up inevitably against this problem: What to do with our ancestors? I mean it as an ambiguity: both the literal or blood, and the spiritual

---

2. Roethke marked this paragraph "Omit" in his typescript.

ancestors. Both, as we know, can overwhelm us. The devouring mother, the furious papa. And if we're trying to write, the Supreme Masters. In this same harried period, I wrote, in a not very good poem:

> Corruption reaps the young; you dread
> The menace of ancestral eyes;
> Recoiling from the serpent head
> Of fate, you blubber in surprise.

And so on... in the last stanza,

> You meditate upon the nerves,
> Inflame with hate. This ancient feud
> Is seldom won. The spirit starves
> Until the dead have been subdued.

I remember the late John Peale Bishop, that fine neglected poet, reading this and saying, "You're impassioned, but wrong. The dead can help us." And he was right; but it took me some years to learn that.

Let me say boldly, now, that the extent to which the great dead can be evoked, or can come to us, can be eerie, and astonishing. Let me, at the risk of seeming odd, recite a personal incident.

I was in that particular hell of a poet: a longish dry period. It was 1952, I was 44, and I thought I was done. I was living alone in a biggish house in Edmonds, Washington. I had been reading—and rereading—not Yeats, but Ralegh and Sir John Davies. I had been teaching the five-beat line for weeks—I knew quite a bit about it, but write it myself?—*no:* so I felt myself a fraud.

Suddenly, in the early evening, the poem "The Dance" started, and finished itself in a very short time—say thirty minutes, maybe in the greater part of an hour, it was all done. I felt, I *knew,* I had hit it. I walked around, and I wept; and I knelt down—I always do after I've written what I know is a good piece. But at the same time I had, as God is my witness, the actual sense of a Presence—as if Yeats himself were *in* that room. The experience was in a way terrifying, for it lasted at least half an hour. That house, I repeat, was charged with a psychic presence: the very walls seemed to shimmer. I wept

for joy. At last I was somebody again. He, they—the poets dead—
were with me.

Now I know there are any number of cynical explanations for
this phenomenon: auto-suggestion, the unconscious playing an
elaborate trick, and so on, but I accept none of them. It was one of
the most profound experiences of my life.

If the dead can come to our aid in a quest for identity, so can the
living—and I mean *all* living things, including the subhuman. This
is not so much a naïve as a primitive attitude: animistic, maybe.
Why not? Everything that lives is holy: I call upon these holy forms
of life. One could even put this theologically: St. Thomas says,
"God is above all things by the excellence of His nature; neverthe-
less, He is in all things as causing the being of all things." There-
fore, in calling upon the snail, I am calling, in a sense, upon God:

> Snail, snail, glister me forward,
> Bird, soft-sigh me home.
> Worm, be with me.
> This is my hard time.

Or again, in a passage Mr. Bracken mentions:

> I could watch! I could watch!
> I saw the separateness of all things!
> My heart lifted up with the great grasses;
> The weeds believed me, and the nesting birds.

It is paradoxical that a very sharp sense of the being, the identity
of some other being—and in some instances, even an inanimate
thing—brings a corresponding heightening and awareness of one's
own self, *and*, even more mysteriously, in some instances, a feeling
of the oneness of the universe. Both feelings are not always present,
I'm aware, but either can be an occasion for gratitude. And *both* can
be induced. The first simply by intensity in the seeing. To look at
a thing so long that you are a part of it and it is a part of you—Rilke
gazing at his tiger for eight hours, for instance. If you can effect
this, then you are by way of getting somewhere: knowing you will
break from self-involvement, from I to Otherwise, or maybe even
to Thee.

True, I'm speaking in these lines of a heightened consciousness. In the early part of that poem, nature was "dead," ambiguous, ominous. But the "angel," an emissary of the "other," was invoked; there was some kind of ritualistic, even penitential, act: "Was it dust I was kissing?... Alone, I kissed the skin of a stone... ."—the inanimate itself becomes alive before the final euphoria of this piece.

The second part of this feeling, the "oneness," is, of course, the first stage in mystical illumination, an experience many men have had, and still have: the sense that all is one and one is all. This is inevitably accompanied by a loss of the "I," the purely human ego, to another center, a sense of the absurdity of death, a return to a state of innocency.

This experience has come to me so many times, in so many varying circumstances, that I cannot suspect its validity: it is *not* one of the devil's traps, a hallucination, a voice, a snare. I can't claim that the soul, my soul, was absorbed in God. No, God for me still remains someone to be confronted, to be dueled with: that is perhaps my error, my sin of pride. But the oneness, Yes!

But let us return to the more homely but related form of exaltation: creativity itself. Can we say this: that the self can be found in love, in human, mutual love, in work that one loves—not in *Arbeit* in the German sense? Think of what happened to them and is still happening. The novel, that secondary form, can teach us how to act; the poem, and music, how to feel: and the feeling is vastly more important. And the "creativity" may be vicarious. Once we feel deeply, to paraphrase Marianne Moore, we begin to behave.

And of all the instruments for verbal creativity close at hand today, the supreme example seems to me the short lyric.

When I was young, to make something in language, a poem that was all of a piece, a poem that could stand for what I was at the time —that seemed to be the most miraculous thing in the world. Most scholarship seemed irrelevant rubbish; most teachers seemed lacking in wisdom, in knowledge they had proved on their pulses. Certain writers called out to me: I believed them implicitly. I still do.

"We think by feeling. What is there to know?" This, in its essence, is a description of the metaphysical poet who thinks with his body: an idea for him can be as real as the smell of a flower or a blow on the head. And those so lucky as to bring their whole sensory equipment to bear on the process of thought grow faster, jump more frequently from one plateau to another more often.

And it is one of the ways man at least approaches the divine—in this comprehensive human act, the really good poem.

For there *is* a God, and He's here, immediate, accessible. I don't hold with those thinkers who believe in this time He is farther away —that in the Middle Ages, for instance, He was closer. He is equally accessible now, not only in works of art or in the glories of a particular religious service, or in the light, the aftermath that follows the dark night of the soul, but in the lowest forms of life, He moves and has His being. Nobody has killed off the snails. Is this a new thought? Hardly. But it needs some practicing in Western society. Could Reinhold Niebuhr love a worm? I doubt it. But I—we—can.

Part Two

Verse in Rehearsal

From *Portfolio* (Pennsylvania State University), Vol. 1 (September 1939).

THERE ARE TIMES when even exhibitionism may serve a useful purpose. Let us hope this is one of the times, for I have been asked to show how verse may be revised and improved. This is a particularly dangerous business, because talking about poetry at any time is likely to be futile and vulgar. These verses have served me before, as part of a lecture in the verse writing course and in an appearance or two elsewhere. It is easy for me to be objective about them because they represent a phase of past experience.

My reasons originally for using this piece were several: I wanted to break down the reserves of the timid; I knew, as a teacher, that students are always more impressed by immediate, firsthand experience or knowledge, even though that experience or knowledge may not contain the whole truth; and finally because when I was seventeen and eighteen, I was desperately eager to see how particular work can be improved, to get the point of view of a practicing writer. In school we studied masterpieces; they were so good they discouraged me.

Here, then, is an example of bad verse slightly improved.

> This elemental force
> Was wrested from the sun;
> A river's leaping source
> Is locked in narrow bone.
>
> This love is lusty mirth
> That shakes eternal sky,
> The agony of birth,
> The fiercest will to die.

The fever-heat of mind
Within prehensile brute;
A seed that swells the rind
Of strange, impalpable fruit.

This faith surviving shock,
This smoldering desire,
Will split its way through rock
Like subterranean fire.

A letter from a friend, Rolfe Humphries, one of the editors of the old *Measure* and one of the best technicians among modern poets, explains the weaknesses of this draft far better than I could. I quote this with Mr. Humphries' permission, at the risk of raising the question whether my poems are not community or cooperative efforts.

> About the poem you enclosed: possibly all I have to say is wide of the mark and not really about the poem at all. But I think of one or two sermon-ish remarks about technique, and will blame you for sending me the text and the impulse. The questions you wrote in hint your own doubts, the first two you can dismiss, and I'll try to meet the query of your third question — "fair traditional piece?" It is certainly in the historical and traditional manner but you could make more use of the manner, and exploit it to better advantage than you do here. If the editors have any intelligent reason for rejecting the poem, it may be that they are fighting shy of it on the ground of its conventional rhymes: desire-fire; shock-rock; mirth-birth; sky-die. It just misses breath-death, as it were; and is pretty trite, at least it must seem so to the conventional mind, almost regardless of where it is set. And personally I am a little bothered by your monogamous adjective-noun combinations: six such combinations in the first eight lines, while each may be used advisedly, is a good deal to ask the reader to endure; or, if he can achieve such endurance, you condition him to a frame of mind which he has to throw off with a most violent wrench when he comes to "strange, impalpable fruit." About that last phrase I do not know what to think, and wonder what you think yourself; my guess is either that you think it a mess or else consider it the central technical triumph of the poem. I am uncertain of its strength either as to sound or as to the adjective "strange,"

[which] by over-declaring, weakens the paradox, or saying "im-palpable" in connection with fruit. If it is impalpable, that is strange enough. I think there is some other word, beginning with un-, a quadrisyllabic word that would eliminate "strange," or a trisyllabic one that would follow it. You have to go, met-rically, too fast and bumpily with "impalpable" to get either the feeling of impalpable or strange. Is all this laboring the obvi-ous? What I think could be done with this kind of poem is de-liberately advertise the conventional by calling it "Poem with Old Rhymes" or something like that, and then work in the idea by way of counterpoint to the simplicity, and have it come out in the end, the emotion breaking the pattern as the faith the rock. Or another thing to do would be, in each of the first three stanzas, hold a rhyme in suspense and precipitate them all in the last stanza, viz.:

> This elemental force
> Descended from the sun
> Is locked in narrow bone —

This something or other else, — and so on, and keep the reader wondering what has happened to those rhymes until they clinch the poem at the end.

Mr. Humphries even made another re-arrangement of this first draft to illustrate his points. Unfortunately, I cannot locate this at present. My own final version, — nothing like his, I hasten to say, — which was finally printed in *The Nation*, follows:

GENESIS

This elemental force
Was wrested from the sun;
A river's leaping source
Is locked in narrow bone.

This wisdom floods the mind,
Invades quiescent blood;
A seed that swells the rind
To burst the fruit of good.

A pearl within the brain,
Secretion of the sense;

Around a central grain
New meaning grows immense.

The poem still has defects: a kind of grunt and groan rhythm, very boring to certain ears; metaphorical rock-jumping, also tiresome at times. The virtues, if any, must speak for themselves.

Of course these changes are only a crude representation of one stage in the making of a poem. A far better way to study this problem is to work with original manuscripts or facsimiles. But these are hard to get. Recognizing this difficulty, the library of the University of Buffalo has begun collecting early drafts of poems by modern writers and preserving them on micro-film. And a few writers are beginning to be less reticent about their processes of thought. For example Allen Tate in a recent *Virginia Quarterly Review* contributes a remarkable essay on the composition of one of his poems.

I have deliberately included the long excerpt from Mr. Humphries to pay my respects to a former mentor and to indicate how an older writer can help a younger. To some people it may seem brazen to enlist the advice of another in revising a poem. To me this attitude seems foolish. The poet's fidelity, as Stanley J. Kunitz has said, is to the poem. In my own case, many pieces are completed without asking for or accepting comment, but I have received valuable criticism, from time to time, from people ranging from practicing poets and editors to semi-literates who profess to hate poetry. The writer who maintains that he works without regard for the opinion of others is either a jackass or a pathological liar.

Open Letter

Appeared originally in *Mid-Century American Poets*, edited by John Ciardi (New York: Twayne, 1950).

DEAR _____,

You must realize that only a most high regard for you as a person induces me to say anything. For don't most statements or credos degenerate into elaborate defenses of one's own sort of thing: into the sales talk, the odious pimping for oneself? And how vulgar to be solemn about miseries and agitations which one has been permitted to escape by the act of creation itself! Furthermore, these particular poems[3] — and I say this detachedly and humbly — are not, in any final sense, mine at all: they are a piece of luck (good or bad, as you choose to judge). For once, in other words, I am an instrument.

But I can hear you saying, That's all very well, old fellow. An instrument, yes. But remember: a conscious instrument. It's no good your trying to play the blubbering boy or implying that you're some kind of oversize aeolian harp upon which strange winds play uncouth tunes. Or, you may continue, changing the metaphor, let's say you fish, patiently, in that dark pond, the unconscious, or dive in, with or without pants on, to come up festooned with dead cats, weeds, tin cans, and other fascinating debris — I still insist that my little request for a few more clues isn't the same as asking you to say hello mom on the television. There need be no undue exposure; you won't have to pontificate. Remember: some noble spirits in the

---

3. The poems following this introduction are: "The Lost Son," "The Shape of the Fire," "Child on Top of a Greenhouse," "Vernal Sentiment," "Academic," "My Papa's Waltz," "The Heron," "Interlude." Roethke seems, however, to be referring to the first two poems here.

past—Blake, Yeats, Rilke, and others—have been willing to hold forth on their own work...

You see, dear _____ , I know your attitude so well that I find myself being caught up in it! But believe me: you will have no trouble if you approach these poems as a child would, naïvely, with your whole being awake, your faculties loose and alert. (A large order, I daresay!) *Listen* to them, for they are written to be heard, with the themes often coming alternately, as in music, and usually a partial resolution at the end. Each poem—there are now eight in all and there probably will be at least one more—is complete in itself; yet each in a sense is a stage in a kind of struggle out of the slime; part of a slow spiritual progress; an effort to be born, and later, to become something more. As an example, look at the development of one of the earliest of these, "The Lost Son":

It is the "easiest" of the longer ones, I think, because it follows a narrative line indicated by the titles of the first four sections: "The Flight," "The Pit," "The Gibber," "The Return." "The Flight" is just what it says it is: a terrified running away—with alternate periods of hallucinatory waiting (the voices, etc.); the protagonist so geared-up, so over-alive that he is hunting, like a primitive, for some animistic suggestion, some clue to existence from the subhuman. These he sees and yet does not see: they are almost tail-flicks, from another world, seen out of the corner of the eye. In a sense he goes in and out of rationality; he hangs in the balance between the human and the animal.

"The Pit" is a slowed-down section; a period of physical and psychic exhaustion. And other obsessions begin to appear (symbolized by mole, nest, fish). In "The Gibber" these obsessions begin to take hold; again there is a frenetic activity, then a lapsing back into almost a crooning serenity ("What a small song," etc.). The line, "Hath the rain a father?" is from Job—the only quotation in the piece. (A third of a line, notice—not a third of a poem.) The next rising agitation is rendered in terms of balked sexual experience, with an accompanying "rant," almost in the manner of the Elizabethans, and a subsequent near-blackout.

Section IV is a return, a return to a memory of childhood that comes back almost as in a dream, after the agitation and exhaustion of the earlier actions. The experience, again, is at once literal and symbolical. The "roses" are still breathing in the dark; and the fireman can pull them out, even from the fire. After the dark night, the morning brings with it the suggestion of a renewing light: a coming of "Papa." Buried in the text are many little ambiguities, not all of which are absolutely essential to the central meaning of the poem. For instance, the "pipe-knock." With the coming of steam, the pipes being knocking violently, in a greenhouse. But "Papa," or the florist, as he approached, often would knock the pipe he was smoking on the sides of the benches, or on the pipes. Then, with the coming of steam and "papa"—the papa on earth and heaven are blended—there is the sense of motion in the greenhouse, my symbol for the whole of life, a womb, a heaven-on-earth.

In the final untitled section, the illumination, the coming of light suggested at the end of the last passage occurs again, this time to the nearly grown man. But the illumination is still only partly apprehended; he is still "waiting." The beginning of the next poem, "The Long Alley," is a relapse into sinuous river-imagery: an ambivalent brooding by the edge of the city. And then a new phase begins swiftly.

This crude account tells very little about what actually happens in the poem; but at least you can see that the method is cyclic. I believe that to go forward as a spiritual man it is necessary first to go back. Any history of the psyche (or allegorical journey) is bound to be a succession of experiences, similar yet dissimilar. There is a perpetual slipping-back, then a going-forward; but there is *some* "progress." Are not some experiences so powerful and so profound (I am not speaking of the merely compulsive) that they repeat themselves, thrust themselves upon us, again and again, with variation and change, each time bringing us closer to our own most particular (and thus most universal) reality? We go, as Yeats said, from exhaustion to exhaustion. To begin from the depths and come out—that is difficult; for few know where the depths are or can recognize them; or, if they do, are afraid.

Some of these pieces, then, begin in the mire; as if man is no more than a shape writhing from the old rock. This may be due, in part, to the Michigan from which I come. Sometimes one gets the feeling that not even the animals have been there before; but the marsh, the mire, the Void, is always there, immediate and terrifying. It is a splendid place for schooling the spirit. It is America.

None the less, in spite of all the muck and welter, the dark, the *dreck* of these poems, I count myself among the happy poets. "I proclaim, once more, a condition of joy!" says the very last piece. All cats and agitations are not the same in the dark; likewise, each ecstasy has, I think, its special character. For instance in a later piece, "Praise to the End!" a particular (erotic) act occurs, then is accounted for by nonsense songs out of the past. There are laments for lost powers and then a euphoric passage, a sublimation of the original impulse in an ecstasy; but—and this is the point—in this passage the protagonist, for all his joy, is still "alone," and only one line mentions anything human:

"I've crawled from the mire, alert as a saint or a dog." Except for the saint, everything else is dog, fish, minnow, bird, etc., and the euphoric ride resolves itself into a death wish. Equationally, the poem can be represented: onanism equals death, and even the early testament moralists can march out happily. (Is the protagonist "happy" in his death wish? Is he a mindless euphoric jigger who goes blithering into oblivion? No. In terms of the whole sequence, he survives: this is a dead-end explored. His self-consciousness, his very will to live saves him from the *annihilation* of the ecstasy.)

Each of these poems presented its own series of problems. The earliest piece of all (in terms of the age of the protagonist) is written entirely from the viewpoint of a very small child: all interior drama; no comment; no interpretation. To keep the rhythms, the language "right," i.e. consistent with what a child would say or at least to create the "as if" of the child's world, was very difficult technically. I don't believe anyone else has been foolish enough to attempt a tragedy in this particular way. The rhythms are very slow; there is no cutesy prattle; it is not a suite in goo-goo.

A word or two about habits of mind or technical effects peculiar to this sequence. ("Peculiar" is not used in the sense of odd, for they are traditional poems. Their ancestors: German and English folk literature, particularly Mother Goose; Elizabethan and Jacobean drama, especially the songs and rants; the Bible; Blake and

Traherne; Dürer.) Much of the action is implied or, particularly in the case of erotic experience, rendered obliquely. The revelation of the identity of the speaker may itself be a part of the drama; or, in some instances, in a dream sequence, his identity may merge with someone else's, or be deliberately blurred. This struggle for spiritual identity is, of course, one of the perpetual recurrences. (This is not the same as the fight of the adolescent personality for recognition in the "real" world.) Disassociation often precedes a new state of clarity.

Rhythmically, it's the spring and rush of the child I'm after—and Gammer Gurton's concision: *mutterkin*'s wisdom. Most of the time the material seems to demand a varied short line. I believe that, in this kind of poem, the poet, in order to be true to what is most universal in himself, should not rely on allusion; should not comment or employ many judgment words; should not meditate (or maunder). He must scorn being "mysterious" or loosely oracular, but be willing to face up to genuine mystery. His language must be compelling and immediate: he must create an actuality. He must be able to telescope image and symbol, if necessary, without relying on the obvious connectives: to speak in a kind of psychic shorthand when his protagonist is under great stress. He must be able to shift his rhythms rapidly, the "tension." He works intuitively, and the final form of his poem must be imaginatively right. If intensity has compressed the language so it seems, on early reading, obscure, this obscurity should break open suddenly for the serious reader who can hear the language: the "meaning" itself should come as a dramatic revelation, an excitement. The clues will be scattered richly—as life scatters them; the symbols will mean what they usually mean—and sometimes something more.

Perhaps I have made these remarks sound like strictures; if so, the phrase "in this kind of poem" should precede each one. I don't mean to imply that these poems fulfill such rigorous requirements or that their substance or their technique represents an answer to anything, a "direction." It is a dark world in which to work and the demands, other than technical, made upon the writer are savage. Even these words come painfully—and I doubt that they have much value. I remember a statement from Jung that turned up in a student's notebook. "The truth is that poets are human beings, and that what a poet has to say about his work is far from being the most illuminating word on the subject."

So, *kind*, throw all this away and read them aloud!

Love,
  T.

The next phase? Something much longer: dramatic and *playable*. Pray for me.

How to Write like Somebody Else

From the *Yale Review* (March 1959).

A GOOD DEAL OF NONSENSE has been written about "influence" in modern poetry, particularly the influence of one contemporary by another—by writers not very secure in their own practice who would have us believe that even their laundry notes are the result of divine visitation; by reviewers of limited taste and sensibility; by anthologists; and by the glib and middle-aging young who sometimes debase the role of *enfant terrible* by applying to the practice of criticism the methods—and often the taste—of the radio gagman.

For them it's quite simple: any alliteration, any compounding, any enthusiasm before nature equals Hopkins; any concern with man in society or the use of two "definite" articles in a row is "Audenesque"; any associational shifting or developing a theme alternately, as in music, is Eliot; sexual imagery or a dense language structure, Thomas; and so on.

A little humility may be in order. Let us say that some people—often inarticulate simple types—can hear a poem, can recognize the real thing; far fewer know what a line is; and fewer yet, I suspect, are equipped to determine whether a writer has achieved his own tone, or whether he has been unduly influenced by another; for such a judgment involves a truly intimate knowledge not only of the particular writers concerned, but also the whole tradition of the language; a *very* exact medium sense; and a delicate and perceptive ear. I suggest that the central critical problem remains: whether a real poem has been created. If it has, the matter of influence becomes irrelevant. Think of the sons of Ben; think of Herbert. Is he any less a poet because he took over some of Donne's effects? Is Auden a charlatan because he read and profited by reading Owen, Laura Riding, Robert Graves?

In a shrewd justification of the referential poem, or less charita-
bly, the poem which is an anthology of other men's effects, Eliot
said, "Bad poets imitate; good poets steal." In other words, take
what you will with authority and see that you give it another, or
even better life, in the new context.

All true, but in some ways a terrifying remark for the beginning
writer, who is often neither bad nor good, but simply, as yet, un-
formed. He isn't sure whether he is a thief or a fake. He may,
critically, be far ahead of himself emotionally. He may be able to
discuss, with real intelligence, Marvell or Pound or Stevens, but
when he takes pen in hand the great models of the past may seem
far away and even absurd, and the big names of his own time awe-
some, overwhelming. Particularly if he is a provincial far from a
good library, or from any practicing poet, the immediately preced-
ing literary generation, or the more precocious around his own age
—and not always the best of these—may exercise a powerful at-
traction. The sensitive young are always acutely conscious of
"fashion," highly aware of the topical, the surfaces of life; there is a
peculiar sheen of contemporaneousness—the phrase may be Hux-
ley's—which seems to exist to speak to them alone. They may be
attracted by those writers who reflect their own confusions: the
roaring-ass "primitive" produced on both sides of the Atlantic; or
they can turn to the overneat technicians who simplify experience
by forcing it into an arbitrary order.

To such a young man in such a state I introduce the following
examples, my own transgressions, in the hope he will take heart and
do otherwise:

THIS LIGHT

This light is the very flush of spring; it is innocent and warm;
It is gentle as celestial rain; it is mellow as gold;
Its pure effulgence may unbind the form
Of a blossoming tree; it may quicken fallow mould.

This light is various and strange; its luminous hue
May transmute the bleakest dust to silver snow;
Its radiance may be caught within a pool, a bead of dew;
It may contract to the sheerest point; it may arch to a bow.

> This light is heaven's transcendent boon, a beam
> Of infinite calm; it will never cease;
> It will illuminate forever the aether-stream;
> This light will lead me to eventual peace.

This example illustrates, certainly, at least two things: a wrong choice of diction; an unfortunate use of a model. The model is Elinor Wylie; the moral is: don't imitate an imitator; pastiche begets pastiche.

One of the great and early temptations is Beautiful Words. How they shimmer, those mellifluous counters that others have used so often. It's the stage Yeats was at when he murmured, "Words alone are certain good," against which can be set Hopkins's "Words alone are only words." But even Hopkins cared for "lovely" for instance.

Now I didn't clutch a copy of Wylie in one hand, and write the piece with the other. Actually, I had been reading a lot of Vaughan, and a friend of mine suggested I do a poem on "Light." I took—I suppose from Wylie—the devices of metaphor on a string —as in her piece

> This sorrow was small and vulnerable and short-lived;
> It was neither earth nor stone;...

which itself derives, I believe, from Shelley.

To adopt the technical device was legitimate: my real blunder was not to make the poem better: it's static; it doesn't develop; the epithets have too much to do; the last line is a banality.

My next spiritual romance was with Léonie Adams—something else again: her rhythms far subtler and more varied, a much richer aura of suggestiveness.

Listen to this:

THE BUDS NOW STRETCH

> The buds now stretch into the light,
> The warm air stirs the fertile bough,
> The sap runs free, and in the night
> The young emergent leaf is cast;
> The leaf is cast, and garish now,

And drunk with mellow gold, the green
Shapes to the accurate wind, though fast
Upon the branch are laggard leaves,
Their shade not finger-dies, but soon
Their patterns swing into the light
And broaden in the blaze of noon.
The substance of the tree is hung,
And all its loveliness unbound,
Its emerald leaves to sky are flung;
But that sweet vertical, the sun,
Repeats those leaves upon the ground
To deepen half a summer field.
And still as dreams that lovely yield
Of shadows bound like garnered sheaves,
A harvest of immobile shade:
But when those shadows move, a sound,
The full and level noise of leaves.

It's the Adams cadence, the hurrying of syllables into speech, as in:

It was my life, or so I said,
And I did well, forsaking it,
To go as quickly as the dead.

The technical trick is in the manipulation of the pause, the caesura, on the fourth and sixth syllables. But, alas, there are verbal, as well as rhythmical echoes: in "Kennst du das Land," this Adams has a line

Knew the leaves deepening the green ground....

While I say

To deepen half a summer field.

Maybe that's not so reprehensible; but she also says, elsewhere,

As sweet as bones which stretch from sleep;

and in "Country Summer":

And full and golden is the yield

and I say

> And still as dreams that lovely yield
> Of shadows bound like garnered sheaves.

I hate to abandon that poem: I feel it's something Miss Adams and I have created: a literary lovechild. Put it this way: I loved her so much, her poetry, that I just *had* to become, for a brief moment, a part of her world. For it *is* her world, and I had filled myself with it, and I *had* to create something that would honor her in her own terms. That, I think, expresses as best I can what really goes on with the hero- or heroine-worshiping young. I didn't cabbage those effects in cold blood; that poem is a true release in its way. I was too clumsy and stupid to articulate my own emotions: she helped me to say something about the external world, helped me convince myself that maybe, if I kept at it, eventually I might write a poem of my own, with the accent on my own speech.

Thus, one can stake out an area of subject matter, hoard up a body of words, even embody fresh observation in a sustained rhythm, in a poem all of a piece, and *still* be too close to somebody else. I limit myself to passages:

> Diffuse the outpourings of the spiritual coward,
> The rambling lies invented for the sick.
> O see the fate of him whose guard was lowered! —
> A single misstep and we leave the quick.

or

> The winds of hatred blow
> Cold, cold across the flesh
> And chill the anxious heart;
> Intricate phobias grow
> From each malignant wish
> To spoil collective life.
> Now each man stands apart.

That, of course, is Wystan Hugh Auden, himself a *real* magpie, with a cormorant's rapacity and the long memory of the elephant. He pillages the past, as in

"O where are you going?" said reader to rider,

from "The Cutty Wren":

"Oh where are you going?" says Milder to Malder.

Or the present; here is Graves's "Full Moon":

As I walked out that sultry night,
                I heard the stroke of One.
The moon, attained to her full height,
                Stood beaming like the sun:
She exorcized the ghostly wheat
To mute assent in love's defeat,
                Whose tryst had now begun.
The fields lay sick beneath my tread.

And Auden himself opens up a ballad:

As I walked out one evening,
                Walking down Bristol Street,
The crowds upon the pavement
                Were fields of harvest wheat.

And writes an entirely different poem. Now whether his conscious or unconscious mind seized on these elements: the "As I walked out," the street, the wheat, the fields, makes no difference. And it's perfectly possible that he might never have seen Graves's poem, or even written his earlier. But Auden, when he does take over a technical device or even another attitude, for the moment, does so with assurance and style. Invariably the poem moves into its own life.

Is this ever the case in my own practice? Well, I offer this as, possibly, an influence survived:

THE DANCE

Is that dance slowing in the mind of man
That made him think the universe could hum?
The great wheel turns its axle when it can;
I need a place to sing, and dancing-room,

And I have made a promise to my ears
I'll sing and whistle romping with the bears.

For they are all my friends: I saw one slide
Down a steep hillside on a cake of ice, —
Or was that in a book? I think with pride:
A caged bear rarely does the same thing twice
In the same way: O watch his body sway! —
This animal remembering to be gay.

I tried to fling my shadow at the moon,
The while my blood leaped with a wordless song.
Though dancing needs a master, I had none
To teach my toes to listen to my tongue.
But what I learned there, dancing all alone,
Was not the joyless motion of a stone.

I take this cadence from a man named Yeats;
I take it, and I give it back again:
For other tunes and other wanton beats
Have tossed my heart and fiddled through my brain.
Yes, I was dancing-mad, and how
That came to be the bears and Yeats would know.

Oddly enough, the line "I take this cadence, etc." is, in a sense, a fib. I had been reading deeply in Ralegh, and in Sir John Davies; and they rather than Willie are the true ghosts in that piece.

Is it an effrontery to summarize? Imitation, conscious imitation, is one of the great methods, perhaps *the* method of learning to write. The ancients, the Elizabethans, knew this, profited by it, and were not disturbed. As a son of Ben, Herrick more than once rewrote Jonson, who, in turn, drew heavily on the classics. And so on. The poems are not less good for this: the final triumph is what the language does, not what the poet can do, or display. The poet's ultimate loyalty—the phrase belongs to Stanley Kunitz—is to the poem. The language itself is a compound, or, to change the figure, a bitch. The paradoxical thing, as R.P. Blackmur said of some of the young in the thirties, is that the most original poets are the most imitative. The remark is profound: if a writer has something to say, it will come through. The very fact he has the support of a tradition, or an older writer, will enable him to be more himself—or more than himself.

In a time when the romantic notion of the inspired poet still has considerable credence, true "imitation" takes a certain courage. One dares to stand up to a great style, to compete with papa. In my own case, I should like to think I have overacknowledged, in one way or another, my debt to Yeats. One simple device provides, I believe, an important technical difference: in the pentameter, I end-stop almost every line—a thing more usual when the resources of the language were more limited. This is not necessarily a virtue—indeed, from many points of view, a limitation. But it is part of an effort, however clumsy, to bring the language back to bare, hard, even terrible statement. All this Yeats himself, a bowerbird if there ever was one, would have understood, and, possibly, approved.

Some Remarks on Rhythm

First published in *Poetry* (October 1960).

WHAT DO *I* LIKE? LISTEN:

> Hinx, minx, the old witch winks!
> The fat begins to fry!
> There's nobody home but Jumping Joan,
> And father, and mother, and I.

Now what makes that "catchy," to use Mr. Frost's word? For one thing: the rhythm. Five stresses out of a possible six in the first line, though maybe "old" doesn't take quite as strong a stress as the others. And three—keep noticing that magic number—internal rhymes, *hinx, minx, winks*. And notice too the apparent mysteriousness of the action: something happens right away—the old witch winks and she sets events into motion. The fat begins to fry, literally and symbolically. She commands—no old fool witch this one. Notice that the second line, "The fat begins to fry," is absolutely regular metrically. It's all iambs, a thing that often occurs when previous lines are sprung or heavily counterpointed. The author doesn't want to get too far from his base, from his ground beat. The third line varies again with an anapest and variations in the "o" and "u" sounds. "There's nobody home but Jumping Joan." Then the last line—anapest lengthening the line out to satisfy the ear, "And father, and mother, and I." Sometimes we are inclined to feel that Mother Goose, or the traditional kind of thing, is almost infallible as memorable speech—the phrase is Auden's. But this is by no means so. There is another version that goes,

> Hink, mink, the old witch stinks,
> The fat begins to fry:

> Nobody's home but Jumping Joan,
> Jumping Joan and I.

Well, the whole situation has obviously altered, for the better perhaps from the standpoint of the speaker at least. But in his excitement he has produced a much inferior poem.

First, deleting the "x"s takes some of the force away from the three rhyming words — "Hinx, minx, the old witch winks," — the triad. What's more, he has become tiresomely naturalistic. "The old witch stinks" — hardly a fresh piece of observation. *Stinks* is a splendid old word, but here it is a bore. It is a prerogative of old witches to stink: part of their stock and trade as it were, and nobody mentions it. Take the change from *minx*, which means of course a pert little vixen of a girl, and carries with it overtones of tenderness; or, further back, a wanton, a roaring girl. And the mink — a wonderful little predatory animal with a characteristic odor. But if we keep *that* in mind, the line becomes an olfactory horror. It's some fusty little cave these two have in the absence of father and mother. And *their* absence takes away the real drama from the situation. It's a roll in the hay, and nothing more.

Allow me another I love:

> I.N. spells IN.
> I was in my kitchen
> Doin' a bit of stitching.
> Old Father Nimble
> Came and took my thimble.
> I got a great big stone,
> Hit him on the belly-bone.
> O.U.T. spells OUT.

Here we see how light "i" and short "i" and feminine endings can make for speed, rhythmical quickness, and velocity, and then, with the words following the action, that truly awesome and portentous line with its spondees, "I gót a great bíg stóne… "; and then the sudden speed-up in the action — the triumphant release from a frustration, I suppose the Freudians would say — "Hit him on the belly-bone. / O.U.T. spells out."

Take another, a single line, which is always a test:

> Great A, little a, bouncing B.

There are three shifts of pace—it's a triad again, lovely alliteration, the long full vowels combined.

Names themselves can be a love—and half the poem:

> Julius Caesar Pompey Green
> Wore a jacket of velveteen.

What's my real point by these little examples? It's this: that, while our genius in the language may be essentially iambic, particularly in the formal lyric, much of memorable or passionate speech is strongly stressed, irregular, even "sprung," if you will. Now we see that the name itself, the direct address, makes for the memorable, for rhythmical interest; often it makes for implied dialogue. Take the ridiculous:

> Oh father dear, do ships at sea
> Have legs way down below?
> Of course they do, you goosey you,
> Or else how could they go?

But you may protest, these are the rhythms of children, of folk material, strongly stressed—memorable perhaps, but do they appear in poetry today? The answer is yes, certainly in some poems. For instance, Auden's:

> The silly fool, the silly fool
> Was sillier in school
> But beat the bully as a rule.
>
> The youngest son, the youngest son
> Was certainly no wise one
> Yet could surprise one.
>
> Or rather, or rather
> To be posh, we gather,
> One should have no father.

Then the cryptic and elliptical end:

> Simple to prove
> That deeds indeed
> In life succeed,
> But love in love,
> And tales in tales
> Where no one fails.

Not all Mother-Goosey to be sure. And the "rather-father" rhyme maybe comes from Sam Johnson's:

> If the man who turnips cries,
> Cry not when his father dies,
> 'Tis a proof that he had rather
> Have a turnip than his father.

Or take an example from myself: "I Need, I Need." In the first section the protagonist, a little boy, is very sad. Then there is a jump-rope section in which two children chant in alternate aggressive dialogue. Then their aggression trails off into something else:

> Even steven all is less:
> I haven't time for sugar,
> Put your finger in your face,
> And there will be a booger.

> A one is a two is
> I know what you is:
> You're not very nice, —
> So touch my toes twice.

> I know you are my nemesis
> So bibble where the pebble is.
> The Trouble is with No and Yes
> As you can see I guess I guess.

> I wish I was a pifflebob
> I wish I was a funny
> I wish I had ten thousand hats,
> And made a lot of money.

Open a hole and see the sky:
A duck knows something
You and I don't.
Tomorrow is Friday.

Not you I need.
Go play with your nose.
Stay in the sun,
Snake-eyes.

Some of the poems I cherish from the dramatists have heavily pronounced, strongly stressed swat rhythms. They are written to be sung, or maybe danced to. Here from *Ralph Roister Doister*:

I mun be married a Sunday;
I mun be married a Sunday;
Whosoever shall come that way,
    I mun be married a Sunday.

Roister Doister is my name;
Roister Doister is my name;
A lusty brute I am the same;
    I mun be married a Sunday.

Notice that the shift in the second stanza, in tone, and feeling—how it goes into another speed rhythmically.

George Peele, that wonderful poet, abounds in incantatory effects with the same propulsion. Here is the opening of a dialogue:

Fair and fair, and twice so fair,
    As fair as any may be;
The fairest shepherd on our green,
    A love for any lady.

And later:

And of my love my roundelay,
My merry, merry, merry roundelay,
    Concludes with Cupid's curse:
They that do change old love for new,
    Pray gods they change for worse!

Repetition in word and phrase and in idea is the very essence of poetry and particularly of *this* kind of poetry. Notice how these poets can and do change the pace, and the change is right, psychologically. We say the command, the hortatory, often makes for the memorable. We're caught up, involved. It is implied we do something, at least vicariously. But it can also be very tricky—it can seem to have a factitious strength. The emotion must be strong and legitimate and not fabricated. Thus when Elinor Wylie writes:

> Go study to disdain
> The frail, the over-fine

I can't get past the first line. There is no conviction, no natural rhythm of speech. I suppose there must be an element of the startling, or the strange, or the absurd. Yeats is magnificent, often, at getting the right tone, seizing the attention:

> Call down the hawk from the air;
> Let him be hooded or caged...

or:

> Come swish around, my pretty punk,
> And keep me dancing still
> That I may stay a sober man
> Although I drink my fill.

Or Donne's

> So, so, breake off this last lamenting kisse,...

In some more serious poetry we see again how the direct address can pull us up sharply. We are used to this in spoken language. Maybe we hark back to the condition of the child when we are being told. Almost invariably a dramatic situation, some kind of opposition, is indicated. Thus in Charlotte Mew's:

> Sweetheart, for such a day,
>   one mustn't grudge the score;...

Or Donne's:

> When by thy scorne, O murderesse, I am dead,...

Or the action itself can be dramatic, as in Herbert's:

> I struck the board, and cry'd, No more.

Or the situation can be given dramatically, as in Kunitz's:

> Within the city of the burning cloud,
> Dragging my life behind me in a sack,
> Naked I prowl,...

But what about the rhythm and the motion of the poem as a whole? Are there any ways of sustaining it, you may ask? We must keep in mind that rhythm is the entire movement, the flow, the recurrence of stress and unstress that is related to the rhythms of the blood, the rhythms of nature. It involves certainly stress, time, pitch, the texture of the words, the total meaning of the poem.

We've been told that a rhythm is invariably produced by playing against an established pattern. Blake does this admirably in "A Poison Tree":

> I was angry with my friend:
> I told my wrath, my wrath did end.
> I was angry with my foe:
> I told it not, my wrath did grow.

The whole poem is a masterly example of variation in rhythm, of playing against meter. It's what Blake called "the bounding line," the nervousness, the tension, the energy in the whole poem. And this is a clue to everything. Rhythm gives us the very psychic energy of the speaker, in one emotional situation at least.

But there are slow rhythms, too, for we're not always emotionally "high." And these, as any practitioner will find, are very difficult to sustain in poetry without boring the reader. Listen to Janet Lewis's "Girl Help":

> Mild and slow and young,
> She moves about the room,
> And stirs the summer dust
> With her wide broom.

> In the warm, lofted air,
> Soft lips together pressed,
> Soft wispy hair,
> She stops to rest.
>
> And stops to breathe,
> Amid the summer hum,
> The great white lilac bloom
> Scented with days to come.

Here we see particularly the effect of texture, especially the vowel sounds as well as the effect of the dentates, the "d"s and "t"s. The first line sets the pace. It *can't* be said fast: "Mild and slow and young." It's a little vignette, very feminine, absolutely true emotionally—the drowsy adolescent; but the poem is not static: the girl moves, she stirs, she stops to rest, and stops to breathe. And the girl virtually embraced by the season that is part of herself.

It's nonsense, of course, to think that memorableness in poetry comes solely from rhetorical devices, or the following of certain sound patterns, or contrapuntal rhythmical effects. We all know that poetry is shot through with appeals to the unconsciousness, to the fears and desires that go far back into our childhood, into the imagination of the race. And we know that some words, like *hill*, *plow*, *mother*, *window*, *bird*, *fish*, are so drenched with human association, they sometimes can make even bad poems evocative.

I remember the first time I heard Robert Frost read, in 1930. Suddenly a line, I think it was from Shakespeare, came into his head. He recited it. "Listen to that," he said. "Just like a *hiss*, just like a *hiss*." It is what Eliot has called "the auditory imagination": the sinuousness, a rhythm like the tail of a fish, a cadence like the sound of the sea or the arbor bees—a droning, a hissing, a sighing. I find it in early Auden:

> Shall memory restore
> The steps and the shore,
> The face and the meeting place;
> Shall the bird live,
> Shall the fish dive,
> And sheep obey

In a sheep's way;
Can love remember
The question and the answer,
For love recover
What has been dark and rich and warm all over?

Curiously, we find this primitiveness of the imagination crop-
ping up in the most sophisticated poetry. If we concern ourselves
with more primitive effects in poetry, we come inevitably to con-
sideration, I think, of verse that is closer to prose. And here we
jump rhythmically to a kind of opposite extreme. For many *strong*
stresses, or a playing against an iambic pattern to a loosening up, a
longer, more irregular foot, I agree that free verse is a denial in
terms. There is, invariably, the ghost of some other form, often
blank verse, behind what is written, or the more elaborate rise and
fall of the rhythmical prose sentence. Let me point up, to use Mr.
Warren's phrase, in a more specific way the difference between the
formal poem and the more proselike piece. Mr. Ransom has writ-
ten his beautiful elegy, "Bells for John Whiteside's Daughter"; I'd
like to read "Elegy for Jane" on the same theme, a poem, I'm proud
to say, Mr. Ransom first printed.

I remember the neckcurls, limp and damp as tendrils;
And her quick look, a sidelong pickerel smile;
And how, once startled into talk, the light syllables leaped for her,
And she balanced in the delight of her thought,
A wren, happy, tail into the wind,
Her song trembling the twigs and small branches.
The shade sang with her;
The leaves, their whispers turned to kissing;
And the mold sang in the bleached valleys under the rose.

Oh, when she was sad, she cast herself down into such a pure depth,
Even a father could not find her:
Scraping her cheek against straw;
Stirring the clearest water.

My sparrow, you are not here,
Waiting like a fern, making a spiny shadow.

> The sides of wet stones cannot console me,
> Nor the moss, wound with the last light.
>
> If only I could nudge you from this sleep,
> My maimed darling, my skittery pigeon.
> Over this damp grave I speak the words of my love:
> I, with no rights in this matter,
> Neither father nor lover.

But let me indicate one or two technical effects in my little piece. For one thing, the enumeration, the favorite device of the more irregular poem. We see it again and again in Whitman and Lawrence. "I remember," then the listing, the appositions, and the absolute construction. "Her song trembling," etc. Then the last three lines in the stanza lengthen out:

> The shade sang with her;
> The leaves, their whispers turned to kissing;
> And the mold sang in the bleached valleys under the rose.

A kind of continuing triad. In the last two stanzas exactly the opposite occurs, the final lines being,

> Over this damp grave I speak the words of my love:
> I, with no rights in this matter,
> Neither father nor lover.

There is a successive shortening of the line length, an effect I have become inordinately fond of, I'm afraid. This little piece indicates in a way some of the strategies for the poet writing without the support of a formal pattern—he can vary his line length, modulate, he can stretch out the line, he can shorten. It was Lawrence, a master of this sort of poem (I think I quote him more or less exactly), who said, "It all depends on the pause, the natural pause." In other words, the breath unit, the language that is natural to the immediate thing, the particular emotion. Think of what we'd have missed in Lawrence, in Whitman, in Charlotte Mew, or, more lately, in Robert Lowell, if we denied this kind of poem. There are areas of experience in modern life that simply cannot be rendered by either the formal lyric or straight prose. We need the catalogue in our time. We need the eye close on the object, and the poem about the single incident—the animal, the child. We must permit poetry to extend consciousness as far, as deeply, as particularly as it can, to recapture, in Stanley Kunitz's phrase, what it has lost to some extent to prose. We must realize, I think, that the writer in freer forms must have an even greater fidelity to his subject matter than the poet who has the support of form. He must keep his eye on the object, and his rhythm must move as a mind moves, must be imaginatively right, or he is lost. Let me end with a simple and somewhat clumsy example of my own, in which we see a formal device giving energy to the piece, that device being, simply, participial or verbal forms that keep the action going:

BIG WIND

Where were the greenhouses going,
Lunging into the lashing
Wind driving water
So far down the river
All the faucets stopped?—
So we drained the manure-machine
For the steam plant,
Pumping the stale mixture
Into the rusty boilers,
Watching the pressure gauge
Waver over to red,
As the seams hissed
And the live steam
Drove to the far
End of the rose-house,
Where the worst wind was,
Creaking the cypress window-frames,
Cracking so much thin glass
We stayed all night,
Stuffing the holes with burlap;
But she rode it out,
That old rose-house,
She hove into the teeth of it,
The core and pith of that ugly storm,
Ploughing with her stiff prow,

Bucking into the wind-waves
That broke over the whole of her,
Flailing her sides with spray,
Flinging long strings of wet across the roof-top,
Finally veering, wearing themselves out, merely
Whistling thinly under the wind-vents;
She sailed until the calm morning,
Carrying her full cargo of roses.

The Poet's Business

Selected notebook entries (1943–47). First
published in *Straw for the Fire* (1972).

IT'S THE POET'S BUSINESS to be more, not less, than a man.

§

A poet: someone who is never satisfied with saying one thing at a time.

§

Poetry: a sense of the doubleness in life.

§

Poet: a constant selectivity; a refusal to elucidate with a mass of detail.

§

A poet must be a good reporter; but he must be something a good deal more.

§

Literalness is the devil's weapon.

§

The eye, of course, is not enough. But the outer eye serves the inner, that's the point.

§

One does not deny even a poetry of comment; little cadenced messages of uplift with the mild factitious strength of the hortatory. They come creeping out of the headlines. *Twiddlers*: so faithful to a negligible emotion...

§

A moral sense can have other outlets than the rhymed sermon or editorial.

§

The things that concern you most can't be put in prose. In prose the tendency is to avoid inner responsibility. Poetry is the discovery of the legend of one's youth.

§

Basis of poetry is *sensation*: many poets today deny sensation, or some have no sensation: the cult of the torpid.

§

Count ideas incidental in a poem.

§

Make the language take really desperate jumps.

§

Talent talks; genius does.

§

Don't say: create.

§

Society doesn't create artists; the artists create society.

§

For the artist tells us what life is possible.

§

Art is our defense against hysteria and death.

§

There are only two passions in art; there are only love and hate—with endless modifications.

§

Not suddenly but slowly words are beginning to take on a new life. Part of the business of the young is to repudiate, which is to do a kind of hating.

§

It is time for affirmations by someone other than ninnies and fools.

§

Poems that praise God must create the belief that God also believes in the writer of the poem.

§

God is one of the biggest bores in English poetry.

§

Poem: one more triumph over chaos.

§

Remember: our deepest perceptions are a waste if we have no sense of form.

§

Puts his thought in motion—the poet.

§

Movement: one of the hardest things a beginner (an honest one) has to learn is how to sustain the energy of a poem: in other words, the basic rhythm. He may have a variety of fresh subject matter, slick imagery, sharp epithets, but if he can't make the words move, he has nothing.

⑤

Each word bumping along by itself.

⑤

These bad-ear poets: their consonants knock one against the other; they mouth.

⑤

Rhythm depends on expecting.

⑤

A wrenching of rhythms, verbal snorting; tootling on the raucous tin-ear, mechanized fancies: his poems have movement, sometimes they slide away from the subject.

⑤

There is a kind of poet who imposes unnecessary limitations and difficulties on the language: who bellows with his mouth full of butter.

⑤

A small thing well done is better than the pretentious failure. If a thing fails rhythmically it's nothing.

⑤

Rhythm: creates a pattern into which our mental faculties fall; this cycle of expectancy calls for surprises. The poet, at least the good poet, provides them.

⑤

A musical ear is a gift from nature: but like all gifts it can be developed.

⑤

My design in short poems: to create the situation and the mood as quickly as possible: etch it in and have done; but is that enough? No. There must be symbolical force, weight, or a gravity of tone.

§

No tiny tinks of random flicks from the invisible.

§

Honesty: the only tricks of the real artist are technical.

§

The great difference between *doing* and explaining what is being done. One can be a conscious artist, and still not have to *explain*.

§

You can't make poetry simply by avoiding clichés.

§

Moments: beware the poetry of moments. Many of those moments are literary, remember. They have a past, a dreary past.

§

Diction: one of the problems of diction, in certain kinds of poems, is to get all the words within a certain *range* of feeling; all elemental, all household, etc., etc. Often a very good figure from another level or range will jar.

§

Dangers: Substituting words for thought.

The sneer is easy to master and usually the mark of the adolescent.

Beware when you think you have found what you want.

§

Description: the landscape's usually better for a *sign* of the human. But don't lug him in like an ambulant cabbage.

&

Assignment: find an odd form in Herbert or Hardy, and write an exact imitation.

&

Style: Break in on the reader sideways.
        Think with the wise, talk like the common man:
                Give noun a full swat,
                But adjective, not.

&

Inspiration: the important thing in life is to have the right kind of frustration.

&

On small poems: a thing may be small but it need not be a cameo; it may be a cinder in the shoe or the mind's eye or a pain in the neck.

&

Poet must first control, then dominate his medium...

&

Response to the image is not free, but controlled by the context. The incongruous response—a common fault.

&

Embroidering a few metaphors on his pale convictions.

&

Much to be learnt from bad poems.

&

One thing that literature would be greatly the better for
Would be a more restricted employment by authors of simile
        and metaphor.

§

Almost all language is dead metaphor.

§

The idea of poetry itself is a vast metaphor.

§

Simple and profound: how little there is.

§

By espousing the simple I do not deny the subtle. The gnomic rather than the sententious.

§

Don't be afraid of the dramatic poem. There you don't have to "think" and you can stand one step away from your cozy little selves, on occasion.

§

It is hard to be both plain and direct and not appear a fool to contemporaries fed on allusions, sibylline coziness, hints and shadows.

§

Exactness is unfashionable; connotative sloppiness is in.

§

To mean what you say—and that's more than mere sincerity.

§

A poet is judged, in part, by the influences he resists.

§

A "movement" is a dead fashion.

§

To learn to suck out the *best* in a fashion.

ॐ

Many famous poems are simply landmarks of bad taste.

ॐ

Despite its effort to be surprising, so much of modern verse
seems tensionless.

Sensory sharpness: lost in most.

ॐ

One of the subtlest tasks is the sifting from time. Some poems
have that special sheen of contemporaneousness, the immediate
glitter of fashion—and still survive.

ॐ

Degrees of comparison: pitches of suchness.

ॐ

Too eager to say what a lot of people will want to hear.

ॐ

False obliquity: the preconceived commonplace whipped into
some shape.

ॐ

If the danger of the lover consists of his restricted point of view,
that of the poet is his awareness of the abysses that divide one
kind of perception from the others.

ॐ

A poet is a goof who doesn't have to bother to think—what the
Man in the Street thinks.

ॐ

The young artist: there is no other kind of mind but my own.

§

Continual writing is really a bad form of dissipation; it drains away the marrow of the brain.

§

Perhaps no person can be a poet, or even can enjoy poetry, without a certain unsoundness of mind.

§

What do we need to know? The history of ideas can get more evidence from the reading of poetry than vice versa. Same with source-chasing.

§

This wanting a background, when one has the whole background of history, or fate, of time.

§

The artist has several levels of life always available. If he falls to the ground with a theme or gets a "block," he can always return to life—to the routine task.

§

Ability to revert to elementary beauties: a test that our judgments remain sound.

§

His method of composition itself exemplified the material: the hunt for the clues to reality.

§

There comes a time in the poet's life when one personality, even with several sides, is not enough. Then he can either go mad or become a dramatist.

§

Freedom has its tyrannies—even in verse.

§

When you begin to get good, you'll arouse the haters of life.

§

We can love ourselves and literature with equal intensity—that's our contribution.

§

A love of poetry that passes all understanding, indeed, that requires all understanding.

§

I long to be a greater failure in life so I can write better books.

§

How wonderful to write with a small pen: the recovery of precision.

§

A poem that is the shape of the psyche itself; in times of great stress, that's what I tried to write.

§

The sense that everything conspires against the poem: dark, light, dinner, defecation. My bones bleed from the harsh task.

§

The poem that is merely painful revelations: my impulse is to tell you everything—which may destroy everything.

§

Did I beat the poems to death? Did I worry the material like a mad dog?

§

The poet: would rather eat a heart than a hambone.

§

I am a poet: I am always hungry.

§

There are so many ways of going to pot as a poet; so many
pitfalls, so many snares and delusions.

§

I used to think of poets as helping one another, as advancing
consciousness together.

§

"You try to tell us in shorthand; we don't even know longhand."
Swallow or strangle is my method.

§

O the enormous folly of words.

§

Move over, sensitive sad minds.

§

Live in a perpetual great astonishment.

Words for Young Writers

Notebook entries (1948–49) previously published in *Saturday Review* and in *Straw for the Fire*.

GREAT TEACHERS are not necessarily systematic thinkers. The very act of teaching is against this.

⌘

For teaching is one of the central mysteries, in spite of its great body of unessential lore, its professors of silly procedure, the assemblers of material looser than newspapers...

⌘

Today I'm going to lecture on confusion. I'm all for it.

⌘

To find out something about your life: that will be the purpose. It may be necessary to change some of your ways of acting and thinking in this course. The burden will lie on you a good deal more; but it also, I wish you to understand, will lie on me a good deal more. It is much easier for me to lecture than it is for me to store up your various reactions, attitudes, keep turning them over in my mind, letting my unconscious, my creative capacity evolve something, make a synthesis; come through with the right nudges, jeers, japes, kind or harsh words which will bring you into fuller being. Crudely put, it is like this: I'm willing to give you a chunk of myself—my time, my patience, my talent—*if* you want it.

The attempt is neither grandiose nor impertinent. I shall not try to poke and pry at your deepest self, or attempt to play the omniscient furious papa, the mentor, the great man—or any of those other odious roles which any teacher of energy can fall into so easily—and still, mind you, do much more for his students than those pitiful time-servers in the profession: the army of mediocrities, the indifferent, the lazy, the bored, the frightened or unsure who cover up their own grinding sense of inadequacy by the austere false front, or those contemptuous of the young— an even more dangerous type—often gifted. They forget, usually, that they themselves did not spring fully mature from the brow of Jove: they forget the vast patience of others who labored for them, often unbeknownst to them. Arrogance, in our profession, is an understandable sin, especially when one considers the brutalization, the crassness of much of contemporary life; the debased ethics of most of the professions; the dead pall that hangs over the spirit. But it is, nonetheless, a sin.

Faith. That's it. This course is an act of faith. In what? In the imagination of us all, in a creative capacity—that most sacred thing—that lies dormant, *never* dead, in everyone.

My amiability lasts only through the opening day. From now on, it's blood, sweat, and jeers. And suppose you do get good: get to the level of being able to publish in decent places, as a dozen or so have done. From then on it's even tougher... You must be fascinated, like Yeats, with the difficult. I'd like to see some of you have the absolutely dead-earnest seriousness, the naïveté, the love of poetry that prompted one gal at Bennington to come up to me and say, "Mr Roethke, is there anything to this?" (handing over a poem).

Don't tell me over again what *I* say: already I'm tired of it. Build from it. I'm no swami, no guru, no Dr. Johnson, no high priest of poesy. And suppose you really *are* better than that. (Oh, I've had them, and even my toughest contemporaries have agreed.) Remember: "The world from earth to sky shows itself hostile to genius."

      ꝺ

Moan somewhere else, text-creepers.

      ꝺ

There isn't time for good taste.

§

We must have the courage, as Kierkegaard says, to think a thought whole.

§

Solve all the leaps of light.

§

The poet must have a sense not only of what words were and are, but also what they are going to be.

§

Maybe, more age upon me, I'll care for the grave and ceremonious. But I doubt it.

§

Poetry is not a mere shuffling of dead words or even a corralling of live ones.

§

Say to yourself: I will learn and treasure every good turn of speech ever made.

§

Plain speech is inaccurate but not plain words.

§

In our age, if a boy or girl is untalented, the odds are in favor of their thinking they want to write.

§

The intuitive poet often begins most felicitously, but raptures are hard to sustain.

§

Transcend that vision. What is first or early is easy to believe. But... it may enchain you.

❦

I dream of a culture where it is thought a crime to be dull.

❦

Give me the madman's sudden insight and the child's spiritual dignity.

❦

Play with it—if you know what I don't mean. The language has its cusses and fusses just like us.

❦

Hopkins... didn't play enough: dear sweet serious man, so full, in spite of all his rigors, of that dangerous pride in his intellectual self. But how could he do it without the pride of an artist?

❦

The Victorians—they didn't let enough go in or go out. They lived in ponds.

❦

Tennyson lay down with the words of the day.

❦

Never be ashamed of the strange.

❦

Those who are willing to be vulnerable move among mysteries.

❦

There is an academic precept which says: never listen to the young. The reverse should be true: Listen, I say, and listen close, for from them—if they are real and alive—may we hear, however faintly and distortedly—the true whispers from the infinite, the beckonings away from the dreadful, the gray life beating itself against the pitted concrete world.

᧖

Reject nothing, but re-order all.

᧖

When were choices ever easy, analyst? You still read as if you were eating the page.

᧖

There's nothing like ignorance to engender wild enthusiasm.

᧖

One of those bright young men who spend all their time being right; a brisk metallic negative intelligence.

᧖

They're almost too loyal to the context: those lyric poets constantly tuning themselves up for a note they never reach.

᧖

The coarse sniggering behind that gruesome sentimentality.

᧖

The literature of exasperation has few noble examples.

᧖

A hatred for the way in which he works: so creeping, pistly, timorous, rank, and spiting.

᧖

The voice box is not a meat grinder...

᧖

Observe, random energist, the bear's placidity.

᧖

Some of these Limeys write as if they were falling over chairs.

ʂ

Love poems are written by the frustrated; religious poems often by the satiated.

ʂ

There should be a moratorium on all poems about music.

ʂ

His ideas were few and very between.

ʂ

Some vast and shabby uncle of disorder: an old dog barking in a cellar...

ʂ

They've sat on the secret of life so long, they no longer realize it's there.

ʂ

O dealer in momentous bromides, O odious ethereal chimney...

ʂ

Their poems are not so much hewn as spewn.

ʂ

The most bitter of intellectuals: he who was once a poet.

ʂ

It's not that many Americans can't think: they just don't want to.

ʂ

The delusion that there is some hidden mystery in the banal that escapes us.

ʂ

The academic tendency to rest: that profound impulse to sit down.

§

What we need is more people who specialize in the impossible.

§

O the lies I have told to my own energies!

§

The serious problems of life are never fully solved but some states
can be resolved rhythmically.

§

The decasyllable line is fine for someone who wants to meditate
—or maunder. Me, I need something to jump in: hence the spins
and shifts, the songs, the rants and howls. The shorter line can
still serve us: it did when English was young, and when we were
children.

§

There are those who can hold forth, but me, I have to holler.

§

Can't we shake things up enough so a high, intense, passionate
speech will be heard? When a long soliloquy will be listened to
without trick stage effects or Pretty Sir Somebody's posterior in
velveteen pants?

§

To make it so good that there will be no actors will ever act it right:
but none can be so bad, in any windy barn, to foul it up entirely.

§

There are only a few bony concepts, but think of the metaphors!

§

The resonant, the orotund, the rounding of
The round full phrases sounding like far sighs,

As if an ancient hill has found a motion
Long remembered, never brought to action...

§

The tragedy inherent in enhancing tradition: to embrace the
dead in the right way; or how to kiss a ghost.

§

Haven't all the ways of being formal and fancy, for this moment
in time, been mastered? Even Yeats in his high speech grates on
me much of the time. How grateful I am to forget them, those
contemporaries whom one honors by doing otherwise! Stevens to
the left of me, Cummings to the right of me—good-bye, Louise
and Rolfe, this silly's escaping to his own life at last.

§

Full of slang, japes, stale jokes, but lively and funny, and sad at
times, with the sadness of animals, moping bears and other things
that live by and below the nose... O keep me perpetual, muse,
ears roaring with many things...

§

Get down where your obsessions are. For Christ's sake, shake it
loose. Make like a dream, but not a dreamy poem. The past is
asking. You can't go dibble dabble in your tears. The fungi will
come running; the mold will begin all over the noble lineaments
of the soul. Remember: a fake compassion covers up many a sore.
Keep more than your nose clean. Abstinence makes the heart
meander. Even the vapors are twitching. Certainly, flesh, I hear
you perfectly. But this time and place is for something else.

Sit here, the rocks are warm, sing the sirens,
Listen to them and your belly will soon be a pudding.
Instead, prance with the cats,
See what the soft woods say,
Let the nerves sing, and the soul, for the time being, keep silent.
The eyes have it. Remember: the dead keep out the half-dead—

Those dreary language-arrangers. Don't be ashamed if you belch
      when you try to sing.
You may be a visceral spinner...

§

The evocative may be the cry of life itself—but what a grotesque
form it takes!

§

These words I have dredged: they have all the charm of aborted
salamanders, an old turtle full of bloodsuckers and sores.

§

May my silences become more accurate.

§

Words wear me away.

§

And every day I curse my bad education...

§

There's an element of desperation in the insistence of the graduate
student's respect for knowledge—as opposed to wisdom.

§

There is no end to what should be known about words.

§

I can't die just now. There's too much to do.

§

Here's to that old harpy who slips me a few sips of the sacred
juice, as well as an occasional Mickey Finn.

§

I know nothing you have not forgotten, young as you are.

§

The wisdom the young make holy by their living: so intense, yet thin, the weedy pierce of pleasure, as a bush bends yet replies, riding the stream of air always around it.

§

The true verbal surprise: the unreal is actually the beginning. It is what we want in the young poet: the fresh metaphor.

§

It's hard to get at 'em. You think you've split the heart of reality— for a moment or two, maybe—and there they are, still bland and decorous.

§

We're not going to split the heart of reality: not until the third semester.

§

Why should discussions disappear, the edge of thought slide so far away, the shade of what we said be less, be less… Thought changes into the shade of light.

§

Hearing poetry starts the psychological mechanism of prayer.

§

The only thing I want to write about is light, what's in the eye and the stone.

§

The words grappling across my tongue, things never said coming across the lip's threshold…

§

It's your privilege to find me incomprehensible. I gave you my minutes; let them remain ours. I hope I haunt you. Good-bye, swan-shapes, dear turtles, witches. An aging man can't tell you a thing. This is only a rage of fat.

§

He teaches a class like an animal trainer.

§

The cage is open: you may go.

Part Three

The Teaching Poet

From *Poetry* (February 1952).

I AM QUITE WILLING to abide by the evidence—the work done—although if it were rubbish I still believe the effort justified. The lyric, particularly the short lyric, is a great teaching instrument. It's all there, all of a piece, a comprehensive act. Even to "hear" a good poem carries us far beyond the ordinary in education. And to write a verse, or even a piece of verse, however awkward and crude, that bears some mark, something characteristic of the author's true nature—that is, I insist, a considerable human achievement.

Let's say no one would claim to make poets. But a good deal can be taught about the craft of verse. A few people come together, establish an intellectual and emotional climate wherein creation is possible. They teach each other—that ideal condition of what once was called "progressive education." They learn by doing. Something of the creative lost in childhood is recovered. The students (and teacher) learn a considerable something about themselves and the language. The making of verse remains a human activity.

There's no point in being grandiose about results. How many in any one generation are true poets? Some may be in a class just to improve their prose—and that's all right. Some may be there to get a further insight into what a poem is. Undoubtedly some of them write because they are young. They may be mixed up, and the poem for them is a way out—yet something more than a psychological excrescence. It should be listened to and, in many instances, honored. I can't share the disdain many professors have for the serious amateur.

It's a departure, verse writing is, from the ordinary run of things in a college—for almost all thinking has been directed toward analysis, a breaking-down, whereas the metaphor is a synthesis, a building-up, a creation of a new world, however incomplete, crude, tawdry, naïve it may be. It will have, for better or worse, its own shape and form and identity—and how often can that be said of thinking today?

The class in writing poetry is a collective, cooperative act—most of the time. But to bring diverse people, including the neurotic, the pigheaded, the badly trained, into harmony is a task that must be assumed, at first, by the teacher and carried on without the appearance of a struggle. One compulsive, one older person who has been overpraised by the vanity presses, can make everybody freeze up. Discussions have to be free and easy, otherwise the whole method breaks down. And often, during the first weeks, the instructor has to bring all his energy, tact, teaching wisdom into play in order to get a genuine rapport, a sense of mutual respect.

Sometimes it is best to let matters develop from work at hand: old poems or new. In presenting these, the author provides enough carbons for everyone to see the piece on the page. He reads it, and some other voice reads it. Often, in the case of embarrassingly weak work, it's best to ask firmly for positive reactions first.

Some have difficulty verbalizing about the aesthetic experience. But often their gropings make for the fresh insight. There is little shadow-boxing with terminology. The problem is to seize upon what is worth preserving in immature work—the single phrase of real poetry, the line that has energy—and to build it into a complete piece that has its own shape and motion. To this task students bring their candor, their explicitness, and, often, their truly fresh and naïve ears. The great lesson of cutting comes up again and again, but the applications are various. The war on the cliché is continuous, but poetry is not written by mere avoidance of the cliché. Little theorizing about rhythm, but a constant reading aloud to hear rhythms, to get a notion of how language flows. Essentially this is teaching by ear, by suggestion, by insinuation. Cross-references are thrown out repeatedly, and sometimes received and assimilated: a rain of examples, often from obscure or minor sources. Why? Either to imitate consciously or to look at and do otherwise. I use a great body of mimeographed material and several anthologies and collected editions; and the University has built special cases in the classroom so I can run to my own books in pursuing this referential technique. There is a constant effort to remind students that poetry is a classic art and requires that its exponents read intensively in all literatures.

Each student is expected to revise pieces when necessary and to preserve successive versions in a workbook handed in at the end of the course. He also includes the results of his reading in a selective anthology of his own making—somewhat on the order of Edith Sitwell's *Notebooks*—consisting of remarks on craft, good lines, poems, anything that has been genuinely pertinent to his development. This is not a mere scrapbook or piece of intellectual window-dressing, but a highly personal compilation, often showing that the anthology can be a creative act.

There are several possible points of departure in group assignments: to play with sound; to work with a particular stanza form; to begin with strongly stressed simple poems, such as nursery rhymes. This last is hardest but probably best if the group is young and unspoiled.

The scheme is that every student pursue his own bent, write the poems he wants to write—and also do at least some set exercises as a discipline. The discipline may lie in composing a poem without adjectives; a poem based on adjectives—or perhaps sets of verbs, nouns, and adjectives; a straight observational piece, with or without analogy; a poem based on a single figure; a revision of someone else's bad poem (Braithwaite and Moult are rich mines of examples); a translation; a poem developed from a first line; a poem of which first and third stanzas are provided; a song (some make a setting, too); a poem involving an incident; a piece of original rhythmical prose—and later a poem evolved from it; a dialogue in verse; a "hate" poem; or a letter in verse.

"Form" is thought of as a sieve, to use Auden's metaphor, for catching certain kinds of material. Even a shabby pattern like the tetrameter couplet will throw the student back on the language and force him to be conscious of words as a medium; also it will teach him how to shape the sentence to a particular end, to get effects with full and off-rhyme, and to manage the polysyllable. He can embrace the form or resist it—either result can be useful.

Every teacher has certain gimmicks, stunts, favorite examples which he knows will work—often because he cares about them and brings to them an enthusiasm that carries conviction. For instance, in discussing form, to quote a poem from memory while walking around the room, then to write it on the board, carrying on an analysis as I write is more effective, usually, than just turning to what's in a book, even though I use beautiful texts like Bullett's *The English Galaxy* or *The Collected Poems of W.B. Yeats.* But it is possible for a course dealing with what really matters to complicated people to become, like New York, too stimulating. I remember a class on the epigram—everybody got into the act: we had a wonderful time quoting ribald snatches from Elizabethans, Jonson, Prior; the more uninhibited Irish. And there was, I think, some pertinent advice. It was a "good" class; however, the "epigrams" that came in later were abominable. Why? Perhaps our euphoria had left us addled. Perhaps the epigram is a form that lends itself only to maturity, to a special sort of embittered wisdom that life brings later.

The perfect example. How we academics hunt and cherish it! One that won't scare the slowest, that is within the ken of the earnest apprentice, and yet won't bore the most gifted in the class. I use, to exemplify the tetrameter couplet, a poem like Stanley Kunitz's "Change," not his best piece, but one with structural devices, a technical cunning that can be made immediately apparent to listeners. It is excellent for such obvious things as its introductory participial phrase, the modifier before and after the noun, the absolute construction, the tercet—as well as subtleties in rhythm and meaning. Another example is Herrick's "Delight in Disorder," with its wonderfully managed epithets and light rhymes, its levels of meaning in the apparently artless verse. Still another is Marvell's "To His Coy Mistress"; in fact, almost anything he did in the form can be used. Or consider Vaughan. Or Charles Cotton. Or Cowley's "The thirsty earth" in its superb plain style. But suppose some coed cries, "I want to write lyrics! This form is for wit-writing." The answer might be a blast of Bogan's "The Alchemist," where the simple declarative sentences make for powerful effects. Then from there the class might move on to Bridges and Campion and Jonson.

At its highest level this kind of class might become like the poem itself, in that the full powers of the associational forces of the mind (or, rather, not one mind, but several) are brought into play. (The simile comes from a student, Mr. Claire J. Fox.) I'm not aware of ever initiating any such dance of the mind and heart, but I have seen collective excitement in a class rise to a point where even slips of the tongue or misunderstandings provided a further insight. "He should anchor the abstraction." "That's it—to *anger* the abstraction"—a metaphor for me evocative and profound.

To be sure, teaching is not the communication, or even intercommunication, of excitement. The test, obviously, is whether the ultimate result is healthy-mindedness, is good work. But again you can't tell. Often, in teaching, the payoff is far in the future.

There are those who say the young have nothing to write about. This is wrong. For one thing there is the whole world of adolescence which they are in or have just departed from, with all its vagaries, its ambiguous loyalties, its special poignance. There are memories of childhood, still vivid in many instances. And they can go outside and look at things with a fresh eye.

My own shortcomings in this kind of course are many. I doubt whether I insist enough on technical finish, as, say, Winters or Humphries or Ransom might. I am perhaps unduly rough on the student who wants a mentor, a Papa. You can't go out all the way; you can't carry their spiritual burdens. I insist that the teaching poet preserve his identity; otherwise he may not only ruin his own writing and thereby lose his effectiveness with the best students, but he will also do them another disservice: unconsciously he will begin trying to create them in his own image.

The conference has its place, but most knowledge of technique is acquired obliquely. One suggestion, one lead, after class or in the hall, if really the thing needful at that particular time, is worth far more than any number of pipe-sucking, pencil-poking, lugubrious sessions in the office.

The surprises are in psychological growth. As in piano-playing, suddenly, for no explicable reason, someone jumps to an entirely different plateau of performance and understanding. A boy who has memorized most of Eddie Guest will appear with a poem, rough maybe, but a real "splinter of feeling."

Most teaching is visceral, and the genial uproar that constitutes a verse class, especially so. It is as ephemeral as the dance, and as hard to localize or define. It is what is left after all the reading and thinking and reciting: the residue, the illumination.

A Word to the Instructor

Written in 1954, this was originally intended as the introductory piece for the anthology *Twelve Poets*, edited by Glenn Leggett. The publishers of the anthology, however, decided against including it; therefore, the piece was published first in *On the Poet and His Craft*.

I SHOULD LIKE TO GIVE, humbly and simply, some general advice on the teaching of poetry, based on my own mistakes and short-comings. I assume a young instructor, in a place strange to him, faced with a mixed section of students, frightened as I am still frightened after thirty-five years' experience, before a first class.

What, then, to do? I remind myself I must

1. Establish a rapport, get a sense of communication with the whole class—and quickly. This means breaking right into the heart of things at the start: making the students aware of poetry as experience, making them hear it. It means keeping as many antennae out as possible, keeping oneself "open," aware of everyone, not just the two or three best. It means hard work: keeping on a full steam of psychic energy from the very beginning—or every day becomes Monday morning. It's wiser to begin with material you know like the back of your hand, rather than start off by generalities about poetry, or by a learned preamble of historical background. Ideally, the instructor should have the voice, the physical presence to present the poem for what it is. Not that all of us are born with the voice box of Dylan Thomas or Siobhan McKenna. But if a teacher cares about what he is up to, carries the conviction that poetry is the supreme art, in language at least; that poetry, even of the second or third order, represents a fast way into wisdom, to the insights of the

race—he will not have trouble bringing even the most diverse class, including the lumpish and the earless, along with him. True, most of us, from time to time, should do some candid auditory testing: find out (preferably before a pair of critical ears) what we really sound like, and even do a bit of rehearsing. The ideal classroom voice for poetry, of course, should not be heavily dramatic or too carefully articulated, but detached, maybe a little "dry" even, so the poem can be rendered exactly, without the intrusion of personality. I think of I.A. Richards, in 1931 at Harvard, reading, say, Bridges or de la Mare, as the closest thing to perfection, in this respect, I have ever heard. Some poems do require "blasting," Donne or Browning, for instance, and Crazy Jane needs her special vehemence. But we must remember not to equate noise with passion. And if your voice is on the thin or reedy side, rely more on records —or let the students themselves, particularly later in the course, do some of the reading. This need not mean, God forbid, turning the class into "oral interpretation." Yet often, when pressed for time, throwing a shy one half-a-dozen lines will tell you much about a student, will do wonders in breaking down inhibitions, particularly if you type-cast a bit: give the student what he can handle. You may find a dolt in discussion with a voice, real rhythmical sense.

2. Wear learning as lightly and easily as possible. It's healthier at the very start to make plain that you don't know all there's to know about the poems under discussion or their authors—and don't pretend to: then you can operate openly and candidly, elucidate with grace and precision, rather than guardedly and arthritically, with all the academic whereto's and why's. I remember Robert Frost saying in conversation, "Let's be accurate, but not too accurate"—the viewpoint of the writer, not the scholar, I daresay. But certainly the notion that teacher is omniscient, or ought to be, should be dispelled immediately and promptly. Sometimes it's hard for a young man, fresh from his Ph.D. orals, to believe this. Nudge him with a name or a poem, and he starts spilling information, often irrelevant. And there are other traps the learned young can fall into: approaching material on the knees (Poundlings and followers of Eliot are particularly prone to this), riding a particular thesis (Freudians,

Jungians, devotees of Papa Kenneth Burke often offend in this respect), or aping the attitudes or mannerisms of some previous teacher, and so on.

But to return to more positive matters:

3. Vary the pace, the attack, the methods of approach. This is of vast importance, and can be easily forgotten. Since, as any competent young teacher quickly learns, every lecture or discussion section, whether of freshmen or graduate students, varies from year to year, from quarter to quarter, the possibilities here are endless. To respect the individual student's viewpoint, to carry in the mind, whether one wants to or not, what a particular student has said or written, to come back to his idea or attitude at the right time—if it deserves coming back to—this I find the most exhausting aspect of teaching. It is also the point of greatest danger both to instructor and student. For the fanatical teacher can overwhelm the impressionable, and he likewise can become too involved in the attitudes, the psyches of the young to the point of his own self-destruction. Thus, more than memory or mere audience sense is involved, and even the young teacher must keep his distance, his dignity, and be content with a limited, a human effort. It's well to remember that even the most fervent can't endure intense lyric poetry all the time; that a class can be a dance, but a course is not a dance marathon; that even freshmen can become hideously expert at text-creeping. Some poems need, demand, a careful exegesis, obviously; others simply should be read and enjoyed, perhaps with a few swift comments, or with no comment at all. And sometimes even the most relaxed, rambling, apparently irrelevant session may open up more than a turgid recital or display of learning. The aside, trivial or rich, or even the gag, unstrained—is often the very thing, alas, as every teacher knows, that will be remembered; in fact, there's a type of student that seems to wait for just the "goodies," the nuggets that crop up from the unconscious. But take my word for it, the canned joke, the studied effect, is usually fatal, particularly for the teacher only a few years older than his class. They may laugh, politely; or they may freeze on you, and then it can get very lonely, behind or in front of the desk, the podium.

One last word. This anthology, uncluttered with opinions and apparatus, will come to certain students at the very climax of their reading years—seventeen and eighteen—when the hunger for the best is often acute, yet vague, unchanneled, or already partly debased by rubbish. No text, no anthology, can be the answer to everything. But *Twelve Poets*—I can say this because I have had nothing to do with the choices—embodies, I am convinced, real teaching wisdom. There is enough here to engage the brightest: to give any young person a sense of what tradition is in the English language. It can stand being embraced, or resisted. I only wish that, in September 1925, someone had thrust such a book upon me. And saw to it that I read it closely, and knew slugs of it by heart.

The Cat in the Classroom

Selected notebook entries (1943–47),
first published in *Straw for the Fire*.

IN THE CLASSROOM, as instinctive as a cat and as restless.

§

A too explicit elucidation in education destroys much of the
pleasure of learning. There should be room for sly hinters,
masters of suggestion.

§

I have a jumbled mind that only achieves clarification at times and
then under pressure, as in a classroom. Then the material
provides the unity; the random insights.

§

Therefore I shall get on with the daily business of revelation.

§

He's got to want to teach in the same way as in the old days a
preacher wanted to preach. Historically, there are analogies here;
many of the men who once went into the church now go into
teaching…

§

I miss the administrator who will hammer the table and say,
"Everything's been organized: we want to disorganize it. We
want intense people who can teach."

§

By suggestion, by insinuation, by intuition—let the material speak for itself: elucidate quietly. There's a shorthand in teaching just as there is in poetry. I smell out my material like an old she-bear.

§

There is a kind of teaching shorthand: a possibility of suggestion which can be far more powerful than the ablest analysis: for analysis is, after all, a negative function... To make them feel *and* think simultaneously. To make the thought as real as the sight and smell of a rose: the growth of the student who can be reached in this way is much more rapid.

§

To teach men to flourish: to press my sensualism into a seed— how can I?

§

At adolescence: so much they don't know; but, in the case of the best of them, what they do know is important and often lost to us later.

§

Those taught to creep become enchanted with such locomotion.

§

Teacher: a capacity for enthusiasm about the obvious.

§

Men are made by books.

§

Very few whose conversation is intelligent or even lively: yet a few who live in the element who can make even the shabbiest cliché sound exciting.

§

There's not enough random energy around here. Nothing but horse sense at work.

§

That mass education sacrifices the best is a platitude; but the extent to which the young, the best of the young, are sold out, are misled, are ignored... The shallow egotists, the empty exhibitionists... the trimmer, the bootlicker, the hot-air merchants, the angle-boys have taken over.

§

If you only knew how cold and merciless, fishy and thoroughly bad so many institutions are.

§

The teaching profession: too many clever men without any gifts other than a low cunning; too many cardinal's secretaries.

§

Teaching: the great crime is lack of a generous mind.

§

Those dear delicious swoons of nerves, praters combining all the worst features of goose and parrot; the patters of their own dung, writhing out tiny noises; instructors of a deep contempt, hucksters of others' talent, rabbits in hutches of misconception, moles —weak-eyed—professors of no love, masters of sterilized ritual and organized self-deception—keep me from these evils, Lord, and the rest I'll take care of myself.

§

Prayer: Dear Lord, may I never become one of those soft-faced sleek self-loving academic eunuchs, from whom all sharpness and cunning have fled, in self-created vacuity.

⸙

He was a man with little capacity for any kind of thinking: therefore he was made an administrator.

⸙

A rat-trap sensibility: slams down on subject, maims and kills it but retains it.

⸙

Teaching goes on in spite of administrators.

⸙

I teach naturally; a student is a supplement to me, like a wife is to some men.

⸙

Teaching: I am against realities at one or two removes, the imposing of the secondhand.

⸙

Richness of personal nature, even without "brains," can produce good teaching.

⸙

Our ignorance is so colossal that it gives me a positive pleasure to contemplate it.

⸙

A curious physical tremor, a thrill at seeing something done badly.

⸙

The secret admiration we have for anything done well, even murder.

⸙

I've had few students who can read a fresh page. Reason: this can be taught only by parents. One reason is that the exclamation point and question mark are the only devices we have for inflection… What we ought to teach is the right way to use the voice. Teach them to read with their ears as well as their eyes… We must teach them the sacredness of human communication.

$

A teacher: to bridge those terrible gulfs that lie often between personalities.

$

Not the boring moments, the small gratifications, but the struggle where we become something more than shadows.

$

All the time you're in here something is supposed to be going on: you're not just sitting there, you're not receptacles, little vessels into which I pour something: our insights are mutual.

$

I had all this feeling of love for everybody and then when I got there, I set my teeth.

$

Maybe in love I'm just a teacher too.

$

The element of self-destructiveness in teaching.

$

The damage of teaching: the constant contact with the undeveloped.

$

Going to Bennington a little like going into the Marines.

§

Cold heart, stone heart, cold-of-a-cold peace-heart,
Everybody to take a piece of my poor quivering sensibility.

§

The harshness of his way of life, the constant projection of his
most intimate self, the dramatization—all these left him tired…
All he wanted was to be alone. In his dingy solitude of a cheap
lamp, and quiet.

§

✓   Teacher: one who carries on his education in public.

§

I like to teach because I like to see people part of the day.

§

Those black hours when he feels that he has dispersed himself on
the air.

§

Gradually a pile of student papers begins to smell like old meat.

§

My frenzied example. It's been a long semester here at Hysteria
Hall. My intense and vexed superficiality.

§

I will recite my mistakes:

    1. I have overstressed the medium.

    2. I have indulged in gags.

    3. I have traded and trumpeted.

❦

I can't abide you unless you talk back. I hope for your hearts. I wait for you. I wish for you. I can believe my heart a certain time. I wish for you, *bambini* of the nerves.

❦

Through the young, I shall recover my lost innocence.

I Teach Out of Love

Selected notebook entries (1949–53), first published in *Shenandoah*, then in *Straw for the Fire*.

ENGLISH TEACHING, in one sense, is dreadful just insofar as it is a profession.

§

One of the principal techniques of teaching is the barrage of half-truths, the throwing-up of ideas to be resisted, to be discarded, eventually. Good as it is pedagogically, it can affect, possibly to the point of damage, what the user of such a method holds forth publicly. His thoughts inevitably will have the accent of the careless improvisation: the mock belligerence of the man who hopes to be answered, corrected, or denied.

§

One teaches out of love: it's an impertinence, an imposition, in the end it's terrifying.

§

When I say I teach out of love, I mean just that, by God.

§

The young are often impressed with a mindless vehemence. They may be right.

§

All essays should be, not trials, but celebrations.

⅄

The nobility of the imagination is my theme: I have to let things shimmer.

⅄

My strength is the strength
Of ten young things: I am with you:
In that first moment of delight
When you look from the page, no longer lost
In the maze of your youth...

⅄

Virtue and poetry cannot be taught: they presuppose a genuine desire to make something, a love, an ear for, the language.

⅄

What's your business? Waking the wits of bitches.

⅄

The most difficult thing to remember: that a poem is made of words.

⅄

Your words are you. You are *them* and not much more. The Description: the fieldness of fields, the weediness of weeds... When is description mere? Never. A freshness in the seeing, an innocency in the vision, the angle of perception, the bringing together of details, not necessarily as metaphors, even, just as objects. Be one of those on whom, as Lawrence said, nothing is lost. Don't strain for arrangement. Look and put it down and let your sensibility be the sieve.

⅄

We must escape from the well-made poem and find ourselves in the material all over again. Don't grovel before words. My task is not to woo you into being.

The splendid irrationality of a peacock's tail.

I teach nothing but the obvious. But that's nearly always forgotten.

That's the horrible thing about being a genius. Everything's so obvious.

The story seems to be that I am some sort of swami who can stare deep into coed eyes and pluck forth some liquid shimmering truth, neat as a fish...

I'll teach you all I've forgotten.

Not to arrange little pieces of factitious feeling.

Something gay and tumultuous, in a yeasty rare high contumely.

Poetry is an act of mischief.

The poem of the immediate situation: that attempts to give the reader the sense of being right in the banal: the problem is tougher in poetry than in fiction (Auden's sonnet on the novelist who suffers dully). The poem should provide that break, that vision into reality which relieves and makes alive.

§

The essence of prose is to perish—that is to say, to be "understood."

§

Realism is no longer possible: for that world has been drained and scoured to gray by the formaldehyde of reportage.

§

The violent effort to break from what is around him in the modern poet: not so much to startle the reader as to startle himself.

§

It is well to keep in touch with chaos.

§

Exaggeration: a lovely thing but it must come naturally...

§

Not a spoken—in the case of cadenced—speech, however grave and beautiful that has been on some lips and still can be; but we need a speech so flexible, so plastic, we're alive to every nuance that the language has...

§

Language as complicated as James's and yet passionate, full of auditory shocks and shifts...

§

The lyric is almost forgotten in this time of sawing and snoring and scraping.

§

A poet's rhythmical energy is, I should say, the index to his psychic energy.

§

In the purely verbal medium if the condition of music is approached too closely, then tenuousness or (if the personality of the writer is strong) chaos ensues.

§

There is much to be learned and wrung from terror, anxiety, fear: there are still "forms" which the imagination can seize from these dark seas of the mind and spirit.

§

Pardon me, Apple.
Hello, Worm.
Here's the Secret
Of Pure Form.

§

Art is the means we have of undoing the damage of haste. It's what everything else isn't.

§

A poetry of longing: not for escape, but for a greater reality.

§

I'd say the intuitive worker might take some hints from what Yeats did at the very last in "High Talk"...

§

So many writers are an immense disappointment: they're neurotic, grubby, cozy, frightened, eaten by their wits...

§

The poet is reduced, psychologically, to being either an ironical mouse or a bar-room blow-hard.

§

These may be matters only a fool or a saint should mention. I am neither. And I carry no more great charity or regard for most immediate contemporaries than the late W.C. Fields; the usual I-can-write-better-with-chalk-in-my-navel reaction.

§

I have said uncharitable things even in sleep about every new critic who ever wrote.

§

Those louts, let them starve with their coarse abstractions,
Let them wither away on their blighted trees,
Dying like dead crows tied to broomsticks...

§

Those poets who go around as if they had just committed a nuisance.

§

They write premonitory poetry after the changes have arrived.

§

Lawrence: there are other kinds of immediacy: so on top of life, he smothered it.

§

A new-bathed man approaching a smell: Eliot toward much of his material.

§

English poetry: mostly by ninnies, capable of fits and starts of ravishing feeling — Peele, for instance — but scarcely capable of filling out a simple tax form.

§

This one ate his father; this one saves his grandmother's toenails;

This one bites his nails; this one is master of the slack line;
This one cries in the dark; this one faints in a paroxysm
        of understatement.

§

Exasperation is one of the means we have of reminding ourselves
that most people are—not dead—but in a milky state of
inanition: a diet-milk the color of putty.

§

Not the stuff, but merely the stuffing, of real poetry. An
anthology of abstractions from one of the less sure
metaphysicians: a nowadays nausea.

§

That editor who bemoans the passing of what he has spent his life
trying to kill: the full free effect.

§

All the charm of a doorknob in a public toilet.

§

These fancy dandlers of mild epithets, graceless wittols hanging
on the coattails of their betters. I can forget what they do until
they forget to steal and start being themselves...

§

They make out by the sheer weight, the momentum of their
tastelessness.

§

He had all the charity of a cruising shark.

§

He was the master of the remark that insults everybody—
including himself.

§

Even a bad piece of writing can have its own mysterious life, and be a fascination.

§

Isn't there something else? Must we have nothing but this leaping and snorting in the dark, these whimsey-itches, small-fry frenzies, silent-night sweatings, yippety-yap yodelings? Why not a dull one-legged dour poem?

§

The doubleness of all things has oppressed me. Gaiety and nonchalance: in verse, in life so rare.

§

The fallacious doctrine that all that is good in writing *must* come at a heavy, even a tragic, cost. We distrust the vicarious experience or do not have faith in the powers of the imagination. Such unimpeachable joy assails me!

§

In my poems, there is much more reality than in any relationship or affection that I feel; when I create, I am true, and I would like to find the strength to base my life entirely on this truth, on this infinite simplicity and joy...

§

I work very slowly: I can afford to be terribly spontaneous.

§

I was a man committed to the concrete.

§

I need the botanist's leaf more than the poet's flower.

§

Is associational thinking just a trick? If so, it's a good one, and for some of the slow boys, of whom I am one, it takes very long to learn.

§

When I think of the time Rilke had, I could weep: and the things about him which tied him to the past and helped make him human.

§

This Caliban of the classroom, old Uncle Hot Poop, a bug-eyed blubbering boy—his burden's made him nervous but he can't relieve himself. Allow me, dear pussies, just a few more evocative squawks.

§

You didn't want to learn everything, and, by God, you haven't.

§

It takes so much time to be fair.

§

Maturity in a poet: when he no longer is concerned with personal mortality… but whether the language dies.

§

What we forget is the effect we have on the young: that we are their lives in a way that is no longer quite realizable to us.

§

Here it is: all signs, semblances, analogies: all teeming, teaming with life and love.

§

Now what's the way to proceed? To snow the future with poems, indulge in every poetic fancy that comes into your heads, or *provide release* — and leave the burden of sifting out the over-peculiar, the wild exaggerations to others?

§

Go thou and do otherwise.

§

When he ran out of material, Yeats invented himself.

§

Eternal apprenticeship is the life of the true poet.

§

We are condemned to singing when we can;
Each long root blossoms to a different sun.

§

The only wisdom he acquired was from poetry: a special wisdom of feeling, not a refinement of feeling.

§

I'm crying for what I can never do.

§

Mother of God, I just invented a few sayings out of me head. Is that wicked?

§

That intense desire to go back to teach them more, to stay with their lives, to have their faces and limbs as I had them...

§

My words are not with you:
I'm only an old tune
Dying on a stone.
You'll remember me
Alone and clucking in the cold,

A mother-hen hatching out some supreme wickedness,
Writhing and seething under layers of wool and linen.
By a voice back of the moon, you will be reminded,
With the deep stream, you will remember:
And I, perhaps alive in a phrase,
Will manage, I think, a laugh
From under the weight of my beard and the moldering
        stones.

The Teaching of Poetry

Selected notebook entries (1954–58), first
published in *Straw for the Fire*.

TEACHING IS AN ACT OF LOVE, a spiritual cohabitation, one of the
few sacred relationships left in a crass secular world.

§

About poetry we can only utter half-truths.

§

I come, a fresh initiate from the fast-disappearing, often-scorned,
harried cult of intensity.

§

The teaching of poetry requires fanaticism.

§

Teaching needs more squirrels, more individuals, more cranks,
more fanatics (but—and this is simply about what really matters—),
more brains…

§

This is the lazy man's out often: I haven't read it; therefore it
does not exist.

§

And then there is the more honest and charitable mentor who
regards poetry as a kind of emotional and spiritual wild oats of
the young, a phase of adolescence to be passed through quickly—

and anything said to shake him out of this emotional orgy is all to the good.

§

Behind the classical façade—by no means entirely imitation, mind you—lives the soul, the crass nature, of a born impresario: his every action, every letter, his every statement comes from an intense desire to be known, to be reminded of, to be different from, to be a curmudgeon—to be—and here I approach the ultimate— a dictator: now this, I insist, is to be resisted with force and fury. Must all experience be strained through that somewhat congested lower colon? Are students, all of them, to be made solely in his image? Does only he hear it? Nonsense...

§

One thing, certainly, that makes for better teaching among the embattled academic young—the last, the real American proletariat, someone said—is the opposition of Authority, the entrenched thin-veined toady to the past, to Harvard, to "values" not only outmoded but obscene.

§

They hear nothing, these stone-deaf enemies of life, literature, and the pursuit of anything other than increase in salary.

§

Poetry, like God, is the subject of too much conversation by unformed minds.

§

The goose-me-again-daddy student, that nose-picking I-love-me fraternity cretin...

§

The Aggressive: these include, alas, those recently discovered by their mother or some addled high school teacher, devoted to what John Ciardi has called the bonnet-and-bluebird school of poetry; or sometimes sweaty earnest types given to hymn-writing.

§

Once a week, take a day off to be generous-minded.

§

What happens is between you and the kids and God, and there's no ratio between your performance and your paycheck.

§

There is, as Hopkins has told us, no royal road to Parnassus: and likewise no one infallible way to teach poetry. I myself am inclined, often, to the eclectic approach: the helter-skelter attack...

§

Don't fall into the fallacy of believing, as many an aging critic does, that the best poetry exists to permit him to show off.

§

Teach as an old fishing guide takes out a beginner.

§

I think some of the effectiveness of my teaching is illusory. I am less complex than, say, Auden, know a good deal less, am and can be therefore closer to the young: they are less cowed, less scared, can pick up my simpler and cruder notions more easily; and have a greater sense of progress. Therefore, to them, I am a "better" teacher. Likewise, the matter of caring: I get guilty about not knowing enough and then begin to "care" terribly. The young are always grateful for attention, nearly all of them—even from a fool, which I think I'm not.

§

Our lives are instruments: a teacher, I exist to save the young time.

§

And who is this middlebrow maunderer, muttering in the realms
    of What Matter?
What aged clichés does he foist upon us?

§

The professor is supposed to know. I am not of that breed.

§

I'm drunk, I'm drunk, I'm drunk as I can be.
For I am a member of the faculty!

§

The nuttier the assignment, often, the better the result.

§

Intuition is one of the classic and great methods of learning.

§

You can teach or encourage *some* students to write, yes, poetry
who can't write English.

§

O Lord, may I never want to look good. O Jesus, may I always
read it all: out loud and the very way it should be. May I never
look at the other findings until I have come to my own true
conclusions: May I care for the least of the young: and become
aware of the one poem that each may have written; may I be
aware of what each thing is, delighted with form, and wary of the
false comparison; may I never use the word "brilliant."

§

I realize: I don't just want to give a recital: or whatever it is: I
want to give a whole damn course: I've started thinking about you
as a *class*—and mind you, in my terms! I haven't been teaching,
and so my whole impulse is to teach—isn't that awful?—like the
old brewery horse on the sleigh ride...

First Class

Selected notebook entries (1950–53), first published in *The Antioch Review* (1969), then in *Straw for the Fire*.

STICK OUT YOUR CAN, here comes a lesson-plan.

❦

Flat words from a fat boy. What pearls are there to cast to colleagues?

❦

To teach by suggestion or "intuitively" takes more time than teaching by precept or lecturing. For you carry the students in your mind and in reading think, "There's a swell example to show Flossie… " To teach very fast, by associational jumps — to teach a class as a *poem* — is dangerous but very exciting. It is possible to build up a "charge" with a group and blast away in a kind of mass diagnosis.

❦

I used to teach like killing snakes: a constant pressuring.

❦

To teach too intensively is to get so involved in particular psyches that there can be an actual loss of identity; destructive both to student and teacher. I remember a student saying, "You carry us farther than we could ever go alone. Then when you're gone, it's too much to face." Let's face it: much of this kind of teaching may perform the function of psychiatry, but it is absolutely fatal

to proceed from such a premise or become self-conscious about
what you're up to.

§

My teaching is a variety of coaching, really: both athletic
and musical.

§

Most good teachers attempt the Socratic assumption of ignorance,
but are often handicapped by their very real and sometimes vast
knowledge: I have the advantage over such fellows in that I really
don't know anything and can function purely: the students *have*
to teach themselves.

§

If you teach by suggestion, there must be plenty to suggest from
—a bale of examples. Anthologies are often inert.

§

You're referee, and sometimes the job is as hazardous as in ice
hockey. Sure, it's possible, with a tweed jacket and a pipe and a
choice collection of polysyllables to hold certain of the young at
bay, to cow them. But they won't be the best ones.

§

We expect the hot flash and we get the cold stale inert lumpish
inanities, the heavy archness, the smirking self-satisfaction.

§

Are there dangers? Of course. There are dangers every time I
open my mouth, hence at times when I keep it shut, I try to teach
by grunts, sighs, shrugs.

§

To the extent that I talk, I am a failure as a teacher.

§

You can't go out to all of them: all the way. That way lies
madness and death. As it is, you work harder than most
psychiatrists—and get much further faster, more humanly,
painlessly.

§

I ask you: I beg you: bring to this task all the sweetness of spirit
you possess. Leave your neuroses at home, and while there, make
them work for you, or exorcise them from your best being.

§

A too excessive concern over students can mean: (1) death of
the teacher; (2) distortion of the student: a sense of weakness
or reliance.

§

The essential thing: that they not be loused up, warped, unduly
twisted, played upon, brought to the wrong ends, led to the
stony pasture.

§

I'd rather just sit around and dribble little bits of teaching
wisdom... one of the more valiantly disorganized minds of
our time.

§

In teaching, gruffness may be the true *cortesía*.

§

In writing you must go ahead; in teaching, so much of the time,
you must go back.

§

I take it I'm to stand up for Poesy, but not say anything to make
anyone nervous. For you know: one of the problems of the lyric
poet is what to do with his spare time; and sometimes it becomes

the community's problem too. It worries people. I know when I came out to Seattle, the head of my department said, "Ted, we don't know quite what to do with you: you're the only serious practicing poet within 1500 miles." I sort of was given to understand I had a status between—if it were Oklahoma—between a bank-robber and a Congressman.

§

Teaching: one of the few professions that permit love.

§

Look, I'm the greatest dumb teacher alive.

§

You think and I'll say.

§

Look how "wicked" we are: we have a poet who's a full professor.

§

A hot shot of the hard word—is that what you want? I feel strangely diffident. I'm a sport, an anachronism: nobody ever told me where to go.

§

I've had a most savage attack of humility of late; the notion that seems to horrify some of you is that you're not only expected to do some work, but actually supposed to teach the teacher. I assure you that is astonishingly easy to do.

§

How wonderful the struggle with language is.

§

The recording apparatus must be mature: complete and steady enough to rely on itself. There can't be any brash barkings into the bass drum or simpers off into the wings or cozy thigh-crossings: everybody hates the unformed. You're a speaking foetus, get it? A soft-boiled egg wobbling on one leg, looking for the edge of a cup or saucer... You roar, not from a true disquietude of the heart, but from growing-pains... spiritual teething. This fledgling's cheep would disgrace a magpie.

§

When you roar, make sure it's from a true disquietude of the heart, not a mere temporal pinch... In the end, if you aspire to the visionary's toughness, you not only have to chew your own marrow, but then must spit it in your neighbor's eye.

§

In this first assignment just care about words. Dwell on them lovingly.

§

For Christ's sake, awake and sing! You're as conditioned as old sheep.

§

It's the damned almost-language that's hardest to break away from: the skilled words of the literary poet.

§

The artist (not the would-be): you may have deep insights—but you also need the sense of form. Sometimes the possession of the first without the second may be tragic.

§

Good poets wait for the muse, the unconscious to spring something loose, to temper and test the promptings of the intuition with the pressures of craftsmanship: they can think while they sing.

§

If only this rare rich ripe deviousness could be put to some useful work.

§

I'll deliver you, dear doves, out of the rational, into the realm of pure song.

§

It's true many of the lessons are the same; in fact, almost reduce themselves to one lesson: cutting. But the applications, the variations are infinite.

§

To be too explicit destroys the pleasure. This the Irish know, to whom the half-said's dearest.

§

I have to be concrete. Everything else scares the hell out of me.

§

Immobility is fatal in the arts.

§

To bring you out of that purposelessness—surely that is a great thing, even if you move but an inch from yourselves…

§

The artist doesn't want to be articulate about something until he is finally articulate. One can talk away certain themes, spoil them.

§

That intense profound sharp longing to make a true poem.

§

One form of the death wish is the embracing of mediocrity: a deliberate reading and re-reading of newspapers…

§

Today there's no time for the mistakes of a long and slow development: dazzle or die. Would Yeats's career be possible in this country today?

§

The "other" poems in Yeats... had to set the stage for his best work. If he had not written at such length, he might not have been heard.

§

What would you rather be—happy or Hölderlin?

§

Much of poetry is an anguished waiting.

§

One of the virtues of good poetry is the fact that it irritates the mediocre.

§

I can't understand the condescension many "professional" poets have for the young. Usually it seems defensive, a form of fear or even a kind of jealousy.

§

Uncle Easy,
You mustn't be queasy:
I haven't forgotten
Cousin Rotten.

§

Behold the heavy-footed bard
With rhythms from the lumberyard.

§

In him all the oafs, dolts, bumpkins, and clods, living and dead, connect and contend.

§

A bewildered bardling: no real feeling except a thin intense hatred of his contemporary superiors.

§

The gutsy, self-appreciating tone
Is something only he can make his own:
The true provincial wit, he never reads
Except the thing his little spirit needs:
I find it comic that he speaks of *voice*
Who never made a rhythm without noise.

§

A great one for hurrahing early work; but as soon as the subject departs from the rude thumps and lubberly staves of the lisping idiotic boy, he has "abandoned his muse" or is depending on mere cleverness. What a burden he bears, carrying the weight of criticism for us all. How fiercely he guards his few nuggets of wisdom. In the perpetual hunt for merit, he is content to scavenge.

§

The critics: they have taught poets much about what not to do— for one thing, to avoid pleasing them.

§

The critic's attitude: this poem exists for me to verbalize about it.

§

A culture in which it is easier to publish a book about poetry than a book of poems.

§

These shabby detractors; these cheap cavilers, gurgling with
their jargon: they're fatter in the head than the worst priests
of disillusion.

§

The pip-squeak peripheral dippers: they could come to a full
circle in the middle of a plugged nickel: it's no good declaring
them frauds: they retain their dubious virtues. It's true in the tiny
areas they leak and squeak in: sand-fleas of the soul on the
immense beaches of desolation. Meanwhile the wind's where it is:
the sun plays in the dark leaves of the acanthus. Locality is
alive...

§

How do I know what I said? Half the time I wasn't listening.

§

I was committed to the future: and in a sense only the future
existed.

§

I don't think anybody ever yearned more for a public than I did.

§

What have I done, dear God, to deserve this perpetual feeling
that I'm almost ready to begin something really new?

§

A profound dissatisfaction with these tin-cans, frigidaires,
barbered prose, milk and water fantasies.

§

If poetry can kill you, I'm likely to die.

§

The exactly right goose to a tired psyche: the Socratic method is exhausting with uneven material; worse with limited. To hell, I say, with the conference. It's enough for me to listen, and cut away, and suggest, quickly. Come up before or after class. None of this breast-feeding.

§

Well, well, have I become no more a dug? Let's have an end to this shameless breast-feeding from one who doesn't pretend to know anyway: you don't cut the mustard always with silver: Any old stick, pie-tin, or pencil's material to beat out the meter of happy bones.

§

We may not be going far: but even beyond the door is a great way in this journey. "I've lost it," he said: the gift for the creative reverie. I no longer listen and wait, but hear only the snapping clichés, our whole life driving toward coarse abstractions.

§

A honey-seeker numb as a bee in November.
To recover the fine extravagance, the bravado, the true bravura...
To find my own labyrinth and wind there,
A placid worm...
You two trees, don't think you're a wood...
My feet leap with the dancing dead...
What to do when the fresh metaphors flash forth—that is
        a facer...
For who would tinker when the muses say?
I call the light out of someone else.
Sing up, sing all, a Socrates of fury.

Part Four

Last Class

Under the pseudonym Winterset Rothberg, this
appeared first in *Botteghe Oscure* (Rome) (1950);
it was reprinted in *College English* (May 1957).

NOTE: In some American progressive colleges for women, it is the
custom to tell all, to shoot the works, in the last class. The school
here is, let us say, Hysteria Hall; the course, The Writing of Verse.

My sins are not important. Whatever I said was too good for
you. I tried. I said and I did. I survived. I have endured you, O mod-
ern girl, sweetheart of papa and billboards; footpad and assassin.
Lord, I'm plumb tuckered out lugging these hunks of pork up the
lower slopes of Parnassus, knowing all the time that as soon as I
turn around, back they'll slip to blurbanity, inanity, and the dearest
dullest people in the world. I'm tired of being a day-laborer on this
canary-farm, a ladies' maid in a seminary of small beasts, a midwife
sweating to effect a most particular parturition: bringing forth lit-
tle maimed ends of life, poems with all the charm (if they didn't lay
eggs) of aborted salamanders.

I'm tired of tippy-toe tasting; peripheral twittering; sniffing for
epiphanies; whistling after Wystan; Tate- and text-creeping; dith-
ering over irrelevant details; orphic posturing; adjective-casting,
nuancing; mincing before mirrors; speaking the condition of
somebody else's mouth; crooning in private over garbled quota-
tions; sucking toes already too tired; attitudinizing, all of those
dreary glazed varnished effusions from the boudoirs of frou-frou;
all the lower case freud and joyce (Anna Livia Dribblenose); all
those moldy little sublimations emitting nothing more than a faint
sad smell; those cats and trees and silvery moons; those bleak black
ugsome birds—why not a whole series on the grave, darling? I'm
tired of the I-love-me bitches always trying to keep somebody off

balance; Park Avenue cuties who, denied dogs, keep wolfcubs named Errol Flynn, or bats and toads with names like Hoagy; all the cutesy, tricksy trivia and paraphernalia with which the stupid and sterile rich try to convince themselves they aren't really dead.

A young girl, said Montherlant, what a dreary subject for a writer. And don't I know it now, me up to the armpits in quivering adolescent entrails, still trying to find something I can save. Take it from me that's been hit over the head, still slug-nutty from those long years in the technique mines. I'm beginning to feel the mold creep over the noble lineaments of the soul. O the lies I've told my own energies trying to convince myself I was teaching you *something!* Twenty times a day I asked myself: Are you really worth it? And the more I asked, the more I lathered, vomiting before Thursday classes, chasing after examples like a greasy stackrat, learning passages by heart only to forget them when I got there, beating my offstage beat to death, schmalzing all day long, —a high-speed pitch artist, a sixteen-cylinder Mr. Chips, wide-open Willie (Just look sad and he'll change the assignment), —I ask you, is that the way for a grown man, and me past thirty-five, to make a living?

I shudder to think of the bromides I've bellowed; the horrendous affirmations; the immense and mindless sense of surprise with which I've belabored the obvious: all that passionate readjusting of platitudes we call progressive education. And by what garments of praise (trimmed with self-pity) haven't I lived and had my being: "Cecily-Ann says you're simply *divine* on Hopkins. I do so want to take you sometime!" Or papa, beaming with beatific bestiality that comes with a hundred grand a year after taxes: "Why, we spent a fortune on psychiatrists, but you really seem to have fixed her up." Buster, I fixed her better than you think: it just may be, in spite of everything, you have a human being on your hands who'll do something more than shake those greasy curls in the cribs of Greenwich Village.

And now, small-fry sadists that you are, you still insist on extracting the ultimate hot-flash, the last tired gasp from this semester-end throe of exasperation. In other words, I simply must say what I think of my colleagues, —as if you didn't already know us better than the backs of your hands; as if you haven't been playing us off, one against the other, watching those ever-so-slight facial flickers for some hint of a rift, some revelation to relay in Commons: "Oh, I know he *loathes* Secondary Source! He practically told me so today in conference. And as for Stinky Retriever!—"

The Faculty! Those privileged participants in this great educational experiment, those members of a community that so honors the creative it just sucks it right up bones, blood, and all. That menagerie of fly-blown lesbians, tired refugees, grass-roots Americans with classic tastes, Bonwit Teller tough guys, drama boys, saxophone players, ex-bartenders, fugitives from the loony-bin; creeps, vipers, toads, critics; finks, louts, lechers, fly-fishermen, sociologists; baby-prodders, pianists; dopes, mopes, coed trolls, nine-day wonders; sibyls, second-cousins, toads, hacks, trimmers; pikes, dikes, perch, and bull-heads; drearies, queeries, vealy-faced fairies; strange little women full of ticks and ethics; existentialists with wet hands; sad-eyed determinists; a professor; stoolies, droolies, ninnies, bibble-babbling informers; poops and prophets.

But give them credit: most of them,—coonie and wide, obtuse, or just plain nutty,—at least aren't dull. Fond of flourishing themselves before the devil, verbal about everything except what they really know, given to thin pipings or furious bull-roarings about the secrets of life,—their desperations, their exaltations are most lavish. They can't play bridge. What they know they know to beat hell: and they care enough to give out,—by some means; twists, grunts, blasts, pokes, shrugs; off-the-cuff; on-the-snatch; down-the-hatch; or with-the-club-dinner. They are teachers.

But there are a few sour specific instances, and we *do evolve* with rather horrifying speed and in spite of all the trumpeting and snorting and parading of the ego, on and off the podium, into certain well-defined, easily discernible types. For instance, there is:

The Creep. A critic. Of the Waltz-me-around-again—Heinie, I-hear-you-calling-Cleanth school. Surprised at an early age, by polysyllables. Mad for myths and schemata. Couldn't tell a poem if it came up and bit him in the behind. A small talent for arranging ideas; an ear like a meat-grinder. There are always these coarse-faced detractors, these busy little men who bite the creative because it is human, debase the genuine truths, and emasculate the language.

They pad through the halls, these insults to mediocrity, their eyes coming to alight only when salary increases are mentioned. They have ideas very publicly, these dreary bores with their clatter-language. And how they keep track of each other!

The Quince. Should have been a pimp or a cardinal's secretary. Streamlined for Jesus, he. Ambition: to compose a great prayer. This God, of course, busy as He is, will never permit. A walk-softly who some day will understate himself into spiritual anemia: he'll prolong the moment of contemplation until it reaches a perfect psychic vacuum. His bootlicking is a marvel to behold: the least possible waste motion.

Bullo, the Barber-Shop Mystic. A lingo-bingo boy, up-high and happy. A great roaring sensibility on the loose: all ear and no forehead. Writes prose. Loves the Heartland. In winter lives on silage. Listen when he takes off.

Bufflehead. A pale, limp worm of a man, kind to his mother, considerate to his students, beastly to himself. He doesn't *know* and he doesn't know he doesn't,—that's his tragedy. Poor dear, he's going to be shunted from place to place, always preceded by marvelous letters which a year later his colleagues will re-read with astonishment. At last he'll come to rest in some backwoods academy, where except for a few embittered cynics and lazy nature boys, everybody else will be stupider than he is. Then, if he marries, he'll become an administrator.

The Udder. All gush and goodwill and guts (girth) a yard wide. A suburban Sappho. The vice in the old village choir. A mind composed largely of fuzz. If she knew what she was, there would be no harm in her, but monkey she must with every amorphous psyche that comes her way. "You can't do your assignment? Try, just try, to imagine yourself a *Tree*." But surely you classic cases in progressive pedagogy, weaned on Freud and Kraft-Ebbing, aren't taken in by such shoddy sex-transfers. What she wants, really, is to keep you entranced forever in the soft silly gloze of adolescence, to have you perpetually saying farewell to the warm womb but never once peeking out for just one look at reality. She loves you best bewildered. Let her be somebody else's mother.

The Allusionist. Do I hear "the furtive yelp of the masked and writhing poeticule"? Is this "the startling hysteria of weakness over-exerting itself"? I ask only answers. From him you can learn the pleasure of tangential authority and how never to come to the point. Even his sighs have another source. Echoes, said Hopkins, are an evil; this man is a veritable cave. And what he won't do, lack-love that he is, to keep his odious skin intact. But somehow he always survives. What's he doing, anyway, in this company of intellectual princes?

Brain Girl. The blue hair and zinc curls give you the clue, don't they? The unhappy extrovert; a female hillbilly who learned to count. So much common sense! And what crimes she commits in its name, always making the wrong decision for the right reasons, professing a great love for ideas but actually afraid of them. A blameless public and private life; a terrible random energy. As an administrator, has done more human damage than a battalion of angels can undo. This she knows and she'll end in a fast car wound around a tree or bend double from cyanide. She can't pray: her soul has disappeared into those hand-painted jars and bottles on her dressing table.

The Raccoon. A lovely man and you know it. His prose would kill you, but, face-to-face, he speaks straight to the spirit. A real source of life.

But I do hear a faint well-bred sigh, a shifting of thighs that means, "Why not talk about *us* for a change? After all, we're the customers." And so you are, dear darling provocatives.

Most exhausting, for me, are you milky sweet ones, still dimpled from mama's rosy interior, braces on teeth, straight from Miss Twitchett's or the stables of Stirrup-and-Halter Hall. Nicknames like Muffsie, Mopsy, Butter-Ball, and Whim-Wham. Some of you are Irish. I can't will such willowy bones into women. I'm not a wet-nurse. What nips and bites you have, little insects for juxtaposition, delicate baby spiders already weaving webs of self-delusion. Look at you close, and invariably you'll skitter away, afraid of yourselves. Ah sweetlings, asleep in your fat, if you don't once in a while, at least look outside, the angels will be forever angry.

Then there are the self-loathers, fond of sitting on thistles; wearers of handmade peasant jewelry in the shape of chicken foetuses. These I have paid the compliment of thinking about in the abstract.

As for you, *Eulalea Mae*,—please rise when I name you individually and when I'm done sit down on the *end* of your spine. It's still growing, remember. From your mother, lovely blob, you inherited the serenity of a cistern. Find some suntanned idiot boy about to get an Army commission. Let him marry your belly and you'll both be happy. In the meantime avoid all language.

Pretty-for-Nice. That block you're always talking about—are you sure it doesn't fit your entire head? You don't *like* paint and are afraid of it? Try drawing with chalk in your navel. I mean: be true to your own constrictions. Get down where your obsessions are. Live with the desperate and you'll survive.

Hell-for-Stuff. From me you seem to want the soft gaze of the brown bull. Alas, my dear, I'm not even a tired St. Bernard. Try a hot bath or the higher sublimations. Keep a stiff upper slip. But the caterwaul doesn't become you. That's a tom-cat's function.

Patricia Jane. In those raids on yourself you have won a few minor outposts. Now pay me the honor of writing like somebody else. I refuse to be best man at your spiritual marriage. An intense desire for experience but a horror of paying the price. To watch from a tent of mink,—that is your wish. But how well you modulate the shape of a sentence and the assonantal sounds!

Ah, true indignation! how rare you are, how dangerous to court deliberately. Have I taught out of the whole wrath? I hope I have. I know you, little unwashed beasts. I love you for what you might be: I hate you for what you are. Yes! I fried you in the right embrace: the close kiss of why not. I taught you as I should; not what I know but what I do not know. I cut you down, and left you singing in your best bones. Did I say *I?* Indeed that would be a monstrous untruth, for I was never more than an instrument. But if only once or twice, some sly generous hint from the unconscious slipped from the side of my mouth, if any of you have looked for the last time into that cracked mirror of absolute self-love, then we have not failed, you and I. We both may escape the blurbs of nice, the leagues of swank and swink, all the petty malice and provincial nastiness that wants to smother, to suffocate anything human and alive.

But before I'm reduced to an absolute pulp by my own ambivalence, I must say good-bye. The old lion perisheth. Nymphs, I wish you the swoops of many fish. May your search for the abiding be forever furious. Oracular nutty's taking it on the lam. There's not enough here to please a needle. I won't say another word. I've hissed my last cliché. It's luck I wish you. Wake the happy words.

One Ring-Tailed Roarer to Another

From *Poetry* (December 1952). It was signed by the pseudonym Winterset Rothberg.

In Country Sleep and Other Poems, by Dylan Thomas. New York: New Directions.

HAS THE RING-TAILED ROARER begun to snore? The limp spirit of a Peruvian prince taken over his wild psyche? Has he shoved down the throttle only to find a ramshackle model of patch-work fancies fluttering to a short cough? What time's the train of his true spirit due? To what wonders are we now exposed?

I say: The swish of his tail's wakened another wind. The times he has stood in the white presence, the muse blowing through him with the true fury! Behold him now, a snout in the sun, father and mother imploring! Long may he wallow.

But ah, where the light is, strange forms of life gather; and what creeps come after him from the cracks, their hard eyes glittering, not lovely like mice, but beetles and toads even God would like to forget: those sea-weevils winding their slimy fingers about him, carrying out his laundry and then hiding it, — May the muse spit in their ears! — those loathly wearers of other men's clothing, those ghleuphs, ouphs, oscars, lewd louies; yahoos and vultures hovering over dead and live horses; hyenas of sensibility; serpentine swallowers of their own slimy tails; dingle-dangle dilly-boys; anglo-saxon apostles of refinement; aging coy sibylline coeds; makers of tiny surprises; tweed-coated cliché-masters; grave senatorial language-swindlers; freak monsters with three frankfurters for toes; sleazy flea-bitten minor mephistoes, playing with the Idea of

Good and Evil,—May he blow them all away with a single breath! And I give them another curse: May they be condemned forever to a perpetual reading of their own works.

What he wants is another Love: the far Son in his eye, not a thick Sunday of white thighs. So he babbles and laughs out of a shrewd mouth, the mournful daughters with him spilling the seed of his soul, praying lovers together in a wordy original song. Holy supposes come out of his mouth and nose. He's bald where it suits the sun; a homemade halo he has in a sour country where at least they love a bard. *And* sing! O the chances he takes with the womanly words as we all wish and cry Never enough of this. Suppose he does beat the last breath from a lively meaning, he never escapes from himself without giving us more than we'd ever dare ask. Was it him I saw step from a cloud, alone as a lark, singing the things we can never know, taking a bird's grace and the breath from us, speaking and thinking with his rude flesh, not a man slowed to a walk,—as if pigs could sing and as God's spy he weeps for us all? Need such a Promethean keeper of fire and secrets look to his meanings, learned and tactful as Wystan? Should we love what we have and not wish for another thing? Here's a great master of sweating who runs and rumbles in and out of his own belly, no staid husband of the dry sad disciplines.

This rare heedless fornicator of language speaks with the voice of angels and ravens, casting us back where the sea leaps and the strudding witch walks by a deep well. May he live forever in those black-and-white dreams, a centaur of something more than he knows, while the white maidens peep from behind the hedges and all the juttiest ends begin talking at once. In a light time the tempter's wrong,—flesh from another dream, ghost on a thorn or high stone, a wonder a wave out far; a full-blown bladder in love, close to shining, the father and son of a smile.

But I say: In him God is still poor.

Wherefore, mother of fair love and the speckled hen, attend him in this hour. Angel of true serenity, nestle in his nerves. May this motion remind him of rest. His help is still in him, more than a trance of voice or skin. In sleep, in country sleep, he comes to believe.

Dylan Thomas: Elegy

Part of "Dylan Thomas: Memories and Apprecia-
tions," from *Encounter* (January 1954).

IT IS DIFFICULT FOR ME to write anything, stunned as I am, like
many another, by the news of his death. I knew him for only three
brief periods, yet I had come to think of him as a younger brother:
unsentimentally, perhaps, and not protective as so many felt
inclined to be,—for he could fend for himself against male and
female; but rather someone to be proud of, to rejoice in, to be irri-
tated with, or even jealous of. He was so rich in what he was that
each friend or acquaintance seemed to carry a particular image of
him: each had his special Dylan, whom he cherished and preserved
intact, or expanded into a figure greater than life: a fabulous aging
cherub, capable of all things. I think Thomas often knew exactly
what each person thought him to be, and, actor that he was, would
live up to expectations when it suited his mood. Often this would
take the form of wry, ironical, deprecatory self-burlesque: as if he
wanted to remind himself of the human condition. Like Chaplin,
whom he loved, he could laugh at himself without being coy, and
call up tenderness in those who rarely felt it.

The demands of his body and spirit were many; his recklessness,
lovely. But even his superb energies felt the strain, I should say, on
lecture tours when he was set upon by fools. Any kind of social pre-
tentiousness disturbed him, and particularly in academia. The
bourgeois he did not love. And he could, and did, act outrageously,
on occasion, snarling from one side of his mouth to a gabbling fac-
ulty wife that nobody ever came to America except to get fees and
drink free liquor; only to wish, wistfully, the next five minutes, to
someone he respected, that he could stay in this country for a time,
and maybe even teach; show the young what poetry really was. But

even in black moods, his instinctive sweetness and graciousness would flash through. More than any other writer or artist I know, he really cared for and cherished his fellow men.

I first met him in 1950, in New York. John Brinnin had written twice that Dylan Thomas wanted to meet me. I found this hard to believe, but when I came down from Yaddo in May, still groggy from my own private wars with the world, it seemed to be so.

Someone had lent me an apartment uptown; he was staying downtown on Washington Square. We sometimes alternated: one would rout out the other, different days. He had been built up to me as a great swill-down drinker, a prodigious roaring boy out of the Welsh caves. But I never knew such a one. Some bubbly or Guinness or just plain beer, maybe; and not much else. We would sit around talking about poetry; about Welsh picnics; life on the Detroit river, and in Chicago (he greatly admired *The Man with the Golden Arm*); the early Hammett; and so on. Or maybe bumble across town to an old Marx Brothers movie, or mope along, poking into book shops or looking into store windows. One night he insisted I come along, with others, when some fellow Welshmen, in America for twenty years, entertained. And then I saw what he meant to his own people; to those hard-boiled businessmen Thomas was the first citizen of Wales, and nothing less.

Sometimes he would recite,—and what that was many know; but I think offstage he was even better, the rhythms more apparent, the poems rendered exactly for what they were. I remember he thought "After the Funeral" creaked a bit at the beginning: that he had not worked hard enough on it.

He had a wide, detailed, and active knowledge of the whole range of English literature; and a long memory. I noticed one day a big pile of poems,—Edward Thomas, Hardy, Ransom, Housman, W.R. Rodgers, Davies, and others,—all copied out in his careful hand. He said he never felt he knew a poem, what was in it, until he had done this. His taste was exact and specific; he was loyal to the poem, not the poet; and the list of contemporaries he valued was a good deal shorter than might generally be supposed.

He was one of the great ones, there can be no doubt of that. And he drank his own blood, ate of his own marrow to get at some of that material. His poems need no words, least of all mine, to defend or explain them.

Five American Poets

An introduction to selections from the poetry of
Stanley Kunitz, Jean Garrigue, Chester Kallman,
David Wagoner, and Roethke himself, from *New
World Writing* (Fourth Mentor Selection, 1953).

I CAN THINK OF NO REAL REASON for introductions except to irri-
tate the reader into attending what is introduced more closely.
These poems need no words to defend them.

A student of mine once wrote in an examination: "I greet a
poem, now, like a living person: with curiousity [*sic*] and respect."

I suggest that if this attitude became habitual with the ordinary
reader, or even the professional critic, so often deficient in sensi-
bility, there would be little trouble understanding most modern po-
etry. For curiosity brings a certain heightening of the attention, an
extra awareness of the senses, particularly the eye and ear, an ex-
pectancy; and "respect" means, as I take it, that the work will not be
cast aside with irritation, or spurned with fear or contempt. For
such a reader, the poet will be an honest man who has felt and
thought deeply and intensely, or seen something freshly, and who
may be lucky enough, on occasion, to create a complete reality in a
single poem. Such a reader will be willing to wait for, and cherish,
those moments when the poet seems to go beyond himself. Most
important of all, such a reader will not be afraid of a reality that is
slightly different from his own: he will be willing to step into an-
other world, even if at times it brings him close to the abyss. He will
not be afraid of feeling—and this in spite of the deep-rooted fear of
emotion existing today, particularly among the half-alive, for
whom emotion, even when incorporated into form, becomes a dan-
ger, a madness. Poetry is written for the whole man; it sometimes
scares those who want to hide from the terrors of existence, for
themselves.

Most of the poets in this group—I except Mr. Kallman with whose work and habits of mind I am less familiar—are the sort often called, rather loosely, "intuitive." Certainly all are alike in that they have not abandoned emotion. Usually they begin from within: the original impulse comes from the unconscious, from the "muse." They "wait"—and then subject the promptings of the intuition to the pressures of craftsmanship. They experiment, but usually within the tradition. With them, the poem, however oddly shaped or metrically rough, exists in itself, alive, an entity, complete and all of a piece.

Obviously, since writers are human, there can be no ideal instance of the purely intuitive poet (all ear and no forehead), or the completely conscious and resolute writer, at the other extreme, who moves easily through the geography and climate of ideas, witty and referential: the thinking type never at a loss for subject matter and a way to handle it. An excellent example of a disciplined intuitive poet would be Miss Louise Bogan in *Poems and New Poems*; among wit-writers, Mr. Robert Graves in his satirical pieces. But Mr. Graves, like Mr. W.H. Auden, can operate both ways. The genuine talent always surprises by doing *something else*. Thus, Mr. Dylan Thomas may think, Mr. Auden may look at things with a close as well as a far eye, and so on.

A word or two about these writers as separate identities.

Mr. Stanley Kunitz has a bold dramatic imagination that can wrest meanings from bleak and difficult material, turn even the language of science to lyrical purpose with speed and style. He has an acute and agonizing sense—not acquired from reading fashionable philosophies—of what it is to be a man in this century. He can break into truly passionate speech, as in "The Science of the Night," in rhythms that go back, I think, to the Jacobean dramatists. To my mind, he has written at least one great lyric, "Open the Gates," already published in his book *Passport to the War* (1944). These poems are his first after a prolonged period of silence.

Miss Jean Garrigue trusts her sensibility more completely than any other poet I know. And well she may, for what comes forth can be subtle and varied, as in her excellent "One for the Roses," with its complex richness in rhythm and diction sustained to the very end. She has a sharp eye for detail, and a considerable range. Sometimes I find myself wishing she would struggle harder to bring poems into a final form; but it is graceless to complain after being startled so pleasurably by such genuine metaphorical freshness.

An accomplished librettist, Mr. Chester Kallman has a varied, flexible technique which one wishes he would put to work more often. He can be blandly and supply articulate as in "Superior Laughter," or more immediate in his deeply moving "The American Room." His *Elegy*, published in a small edition by the Tibor de Nagy Gallery (1951), is one of the readable longer poems of our time.

The very young today rarely "sing," in the lyrical outburst, the song. Mr. David Wagoner can, and does, in "Pause." He has an eye, too, as well as an ear; and what is often rare in the lyrical poet, a real awareness and knowledge of people.

Let me say that the writers in this group represent no new school or special coterie of friends. They are simply poets, writing at this time, who usually go their own way; have hearts and minds; trust in themselves and the imagination of the race. There are others, and many, like and unlike them. Let me say that, apart from myself, each of them, at least once, makes the language really come off, makes the poem happen. And for this, the ordinary reader, the sophisticated reader, the obtuse or sensitive critic, the fierce young, can have but one reaction: simple gratitude.

The Poetry of Louise Bogan

From the *Critical Quarterly* (Summer 1961).

TWO OF THE CHARGES most frequently leveled against poetry by women are a lack of range—in subject matter, in emotional tone—and lack of a sense of humor. And one could, in individual instances among writers of real talent, add other aesthetic and moral shortcomings: the spinning-out; the embroidering of trivial themes; a concern with the mere surfaces of life—that special province of the feminine talent in prose—hiding from the real agonies of the spirit; refusing to face up to what existence is; lyric or religious posturing; running between the boudoir and the altar, stamping a tiny foot against God; or lapsing into a sententiousness that implies the author has re-invented integrity; carrying on excessively about Fate, about time; lamenting the lot of the woman; caterwauling; writing the same poem about fifty times, and so on.

But Louise Bogan is something else. True, a very few of her earliest poems bear the mark of fashion, but for the most part she writes out of the severest lyrical tradition in English. Her real spiritual ancestors are Campion, Jonson, the anonymous Elizabethan song writers. The word order is usually direct, the plunge straight into the subject, the music rich and subtle (she has one of the best ears of our time), and the subject invariably given its due and no more. As a result, her poems, even the less consequential, have a finality, a comprehensiveness, the sense of being all of a piece, that we demand from the short poem at its best.

The body of her complete poetic work is not great, but the "range," both emotional and geographical, is much wider than might be expected from a lyric poet. There is the brilliant (and exact) imagery of her New England childhood; there is also the highly formal world of Swift's Ireland; the rich and baroque

background of Italy called up in the evocative "Italian Morning."
And, of course, her beloved Austria. Her best lyrics, unlike so much
American work, have the sense of a civilization behind them—and
this without the deliberate piling up of exotic details, or the taking
over of a special, say Grecian, vocabulary.

Invariably these effects are produced with great economy, with
the exact sense of diction that is one of the special marks of her
style. Even out of context, their power, I believe, is evident. Thus,
in "Hypocrite Swift," a curious tour de force which incorporates
many actual phrases from Swift's *Journal to Stella*, there suddenly
occurs the stanza:

> On walls at court, long gilded mirrors gaze.
> The parquet shines; outside the snow falls deep.
> Venus, the Muses stare above the maze.
> Now sleep.

For one terrifying instant we are within Swift's mind, in eigh-
teenth-century Ireland, sharing the glitter, the horror and glory of
his madness.

Again, from the poem "Italian Morning," the lines:

> The big magnolia, like a hand,
> Repeats our flesh. (O bred to love,
> Gathered to silence!) In a land
> Thus garnished, there is time enough
>
> To pace the rooms where painted swags
> Of fruit and flower in pride depend,
> Stayed as we are not.

The "garnished" and the "painted swags" are triumphs of exac-
titude in language; they suggest the elaborate background without
recourse to merely baroque diction.

This is only one, and by no means the best, of Miss Bogan's
poems on time, on change, on the cessation of time. Even in her
earliest work, she seems to be seeking a moment when things are
caught, fixed, frozen, seen, for an instant, under the eye of eternity.

A very early piece, "Decoration," printed in her first book, *Body of This Death*, but not in the Collected, is, I believe, a beginning, a groping toward this central theme:

A macaw preens upon a branch outspread
With jewelry of seed. He's deaf and mute.
The sky behind him splits like gorgeous fruit
And claw-like leaves clutch light till it has bled.
The raw diagonal bounty of his wings
Scrapes on the eye color too chafed. He beats
A flattered tail out against gauzy heats;
He has the frustrate look of cheated kings.
And all the simple evening passes by:
A gillyflower spans its little height
And lovers with their mouths press out their grief.
The bird fans wide his striped regality
Prismatic, while against a sky breath-white
A crystal tree lets fall a crystal leaf.

This is a vulnerable poem, in spite of certain felicities (the fine "and all the simple evening passes by," for instance). But the uncharitable might say hardly beyond magazine verse. And even though Miss Bogan disarms us with her title, the poem remains too static, not very interesting syntactically, and the final line plays upon one of the clichés of the twenties: "A crystal tree lets fall a crystal leaf." Still, the scene is looked at steadily and closely: the poem is what it is.

Another early piece, "Statue and Birds," is already a much better poem on essentially the same theme. However, the "Medusa," printed on the page opposite "Decoration" in the first book, is a breakthrough to great poetry, the whole piece welling up from the unconscious, dictated as it were.

I had come to the house, in a cave of trees,
Facing a sheer sky.
Everything moved, — a bell hung ready to strike,
Sun and reflection wheeled by.

When the bare eyes were before me
And the hissing hair,
Held up at a window, seen through a door.

The stiff bald eyes, the serpents on the forehead
Formed in the air.

This is a dead scene forever now.
Nothing will ever stir.
The end will never brighten it more than this,
Nor the rain blur.

The water will always fall, and will not fall,
And the tipped bell make no sound.
The grass will always be growing for hay
Deep on the ground.

And I shall stand here like a shadow
Under the great balanced day,
My eyes on the yellow dust, that was lifting in the wind,
And does not drift away.

Now, what does this poem mean?—in final terms? It could be regarded, simply, as a poem of hallucination—a rare enough thing —that maintains its hold on the reader from the very opening lines to the end. But we are told some other things, with the repetitiousness of obsession: "I had come to the house, in a cave of trees": the house itself is in a cave, a womb within a womb, as it were. But notice: "Facing a sheer sky"—obviously the "scene" is being played against a backdrop of heaven, of eternity, with everything moving yet not moving—"a bell hung ready to strike."

Then the terrifying moment: "the bare eyes," "the hissing hair," of the anima, the Medusa, the man-in-the-woman, mother— her mother, possibly—again "Held up at a window," "seen through a door": certainly feminine symbols. And notice, "The stiff bald eyes, the serpents on the forehead / Formed in the air"—in erectus, in other words.

The last three stanzas bring us the self-revelation, the terrible finality of the ultimately traumatic experience. I shan't labor the interpretation further, except—why "yellow dust"? To me, it suggests the sulphurous fires of hell, here under the sheer sky of eternity.

I suggest that this is a great lyric and in an area of experience where most writers are afraid to go—or are incapable of going.

Miss Bogan is a contender, an opponent, an adversary, whether it be the devouring or overpowering mother, or time itself. And she can quarrel with her daemon, her other self, as in "Come, Break with Time." Here she manages with great skill the hortatory tone, the command, from which so much bogus poetry often results.

> Come, break with time,
> You who were lorded
> By a clock's chime
> So ill afforded.
> If time is allayed
> Be not afraid.
>
> *I shall break, if I will.*
> Break, since you must.
> Time has its fill,
> Sated with dust.
> Long the clock's hand
> Burned like a brand.
>
> Take the rocks' speed
> And earth's heavy measure.
> Let buried seed
> Drain out time's pleasure,
> Take time's decrees.
> Come, cruel ease.

Notice the remarkable shift in rhythm in the last stanza, with the run-on lines that pick up the momentum of the poem. We are caught up in the earth's whole movement; I am reminded, perhaps eccentrically, of Wordsworth's

> No motion has she now, no force;
> She neither hears nor sees;
> Rolled round in earth's diurnal course,
> With rocks, and stones, and trees.

In this instance, I feel one poem supports, gives additional credence, to the other.

Yet Miss Bogan does not rest with that effect. There is a terrible irony in "Let buried seed / Drain out time's pleasure." Then the acceptance that all humans must make: "Take time's decrees." The last line remains for me a powerful ambiguity. Is she like Cleopatra, or Keats, asking for easeful death, or the cruel ease of unawareness, of insentience, of the relief from time that old age provides? There is, of course, no final answer, and none is necessary.

One definition of serious lyric—it may come from Stanley Kunitz—would call it a revelation of a tragic personality. Behind the Bogan poems is a woman intense, proud, strong-willed, never hysterical or silly; who scorns the open unabashed caterwaul so usual with the love poet, male or female; who never writes a serious poem until there is a genuine "up-welling" from the unconscious; who shapes emotion into an inevitable-seeming, an endurable, form.

For love, passion, its complexities, its tensions, its betrayals, is one of Louise Bogan's chief themes. And this love, along with marriage itself, is a virtual battle-ground. But the enemy is respected, the other is there, given his due; the experience, whatever its difficulties, shared.

Thus, in "Old Countryside":

> Beyond the hour we counted rain that fell
> On the slanted shutter, all has come to proof.
> The summer thunder, like a wooden bell,
> Rang in the storm above the mansard roof,
>
> And mirrors cast the cloudy day along
> The attic floor; wind made the clapboards creak.
> You braced against the wall to make it strong,
> A shell against your cheek.
>
> Long since, we pulled brown oak-leaves to the ground
> In a winter of dry trees; we heard the cock
> Shout its unplaceable cry, the axe's sound
> Delay a moment after the axe's stroke.
>
> Far back, we saw, in the stillest of the year,
> The scrawled vine shudder, and the rose-branch show
> Red to the thorns, and, sharp as sight can bear,
> The thin hound's body arched against the snow.

This, it need hardly be said, is typical Bogan: the concern with time, the setting put down with great exactitude, the event re-created and then looked back upon—the whole thing vivid in the mind's eye, in the memory. The details are no mere accretion, but are developed with a cumulative surprise and the power of great art.

Notice the oracular, almost Shakespearean finality of "all has come to proof"—and this, at the start of a poem. She announces boldly but not portentously, and we believe. Notice, too, the mastery of the epithet—the cock's "unplaceable cry," the "scrawled vine," the rose-branch "red to the thorns." And then the final triumph of the last image, upon which everything hinges. "The thin hound's body arched against the snow."

But what has come to proof? We are not told, explicitly, nor should we be. Invariably, the final experience, however vivid and exact the imagery, comes to us obliquely. It stays with us, can be brooded upon, and brought, finally, into our lives.

This obliquity, at once both Puritan and feminine, brings Louise Bogan close, despite differences in temperament, to Emily Dickinson and to Marianne Moore. None quails before the eye of eternity; their world is their own, sharply defined. If others enter it, the arrival, the meeting, is on their terms.

Many of the best Bogan poems in this vein are of such complexity and depth that the excerpt is virtually impossible, particularly since Miss Bogan often employs the single developed image with usually at least two levels of meaning. And often, within a very short space, she effects an almost intolerable tension, a crescendo in rhythm, as in "Men Loved Wholly Beyond Wisdom"; or builds up the theme powerfully, as in the remarkable "Feuer-Nacht," and then takes a chance with a generalization without losing the momentum of the poem:

> To touch at the sedge
> And then run tame
> Is a broken pledge.
> The leaf-shaped flame
> Shears the bark piled for winter,
> The grass in the stall.
> Sworn to lick at a little,
> It has burned all.

Some of her best pieces begin with the object perceived, as it were, for an instant, and the image remembered, fixed in the mind unforgettably.

However, she is not, as I have said, a poet of the immediate moment, as say, Lawrence, but of the time after, when things come into their true focus, into the resolution, the final perspective. Listen to "Roman Fountain":

> Up from the bronze, I saw
> Water without a flaw
> Rush to its rest in air,
> Reach to its rest, and fall.
>
> Bronze of the blackest shade,
> An element man-made,
> Shaping upright the bare
> Clear gouts of water in air.
>
> O, as with arm and hammer,
> Still it is good to strive
> To beat out the image whole,
> To echo the shout and stammer
> When full-gushed waters, alive,
> Strike on the fountain's bowl
> After the air of summer.

For me, the opening lines are one of the great felicities of our time: the thing put down with an ultimate exactness, absolutely as it is. Perhaps the two appositives "Bronze of the blackest shade, / An element man-made" in the next stanza are a bit "written"; but "gouts of water" saves everything. Nor do I care much for the evocative outcry—and the arm and hammer image. Yet the poem resolves itself with characteristic candor. We have come a long way in a short space.

I believe this poem will stay in the language: its opening alone demands immortality. Yet it exists, too, as a superb piece of observation; as a phallic poem; as a poem about the nature of the creative act in the no-longer young artist.

In the last lines of the piece, we hear the accent of the later work: a tone of resignation, an acceptance of middle age, a comment, often, on the ironies of circumstance. Of these, I believe "Henceforth, from the Mind" to be a masterpiece, a poem that could be set beside the best work of the Elizabethans:

> Henceforth, from the mind,
> For your whole joy, must spring
> Such joy as you may find
> In any earthly thing,
> And every time and place
> Will take your thought for grace.
>
> Henceforth, from the tongue,
> From shallow speech alone,
> Comes joy you thought, when young,
> Would wring you to the bone,
> Would pierce you to the heart
> And spoil its stop and start.
>
> Henceforward, from the shell,
> Wherein you heard, and wondered
> At oceans like a bell
> So far from ocean sundered—
> A smothered sound that sleeps
> Long lost within lost deeps,
>
> Will chime you change and hours,
> The shadow of increase,
> Will sound you flowers
> Born under troubled peace—
> Henceforth, henceforth
> Will echo sea and earth.

And certainly, "Song," "Homunculus," and "Kept," at the very least, are among our best short lyrics. We are told:

> Time for the pretty clay,
> Time for the straw, the wood.
> The playthings of the young
> Get broken in the play,
> Get broken, as they should.

And, in terms of personal revelation, "The Dream" might be re-
garded as a later companion piece to "Medusa." In some of these
last poems, as "After the Persian," "Song for the Last Act," the
rhythms, the music, are richly modulated, highly stylized, grave and
slow. Miss Bogan is not repeating herself, but moving into another
world. There is no lessening of her powers.

I find my rather simple method of "pointing out"—at which
Miss Marianne Moore is such a master—has omitted or underem-
phasized certain qualities in Louise Bogan's work, and of necessity
passed by remarkable poems.

For example, the great variety and surety of her rhythms—that
clue to the energy of the psyche. Usually the movement of the
poem is established in the very first lines, as it should be:

> If ever I render back your heart,
> So long to me delight and plunder,

or

> To me, one silly task is like another.
> I bare the shambling tricks of lust and pride.

And she is a master of texture, yet always the line is kept firm:
she does not lapse into "sound" for the sake of sound, lest the poem
thin out into loose "incantatory" effects. Thus:

> Under the thunder-dark, the cicadas resound

or the grave rhythm of

> The measured blood beats out the year's delay

or in "Winter Swan":

> It is a hollow garden, under the cloud;
> Beneath the heel a hollow earth is turned;
> Within the mind the live blood shouts aloud;
> Under the breast the willing blood is burned,
> Shut with the fire passed and the fire returned.

Louise Bogan rarely, if ever, repeats a cadence, and this in an age
when some poets achieve considerable reputation with two or three

or even one rhythm. The reason for this is, I believe, her absolute loyalty to the particular emotion, which can range from the wry tenderness and humor of "The Crossed Apple" to the vehemence of "Several Voices Out of a Cloud":

> Come, drunks and drug-takers; come, perverts unnerved!
> Receive the laurel, given, though late, on merit; to whom and
> > wherever deserved.
>
> Parochial punks, trimmers, nice people, joiners true-blue,
> Get the hell out of the way of the laurel. It is deathless
> > And it isn't for you.

This, for me, incorporates the truly savage indignation of Swift —and still manages to be really funny. And even in a poem on a "high" theme, "I Saw Eternity," she can say:

> Here, mice, rats,
> Porcupines and toads,
> Moles, shrews, squirrels,
> Weasels, turtles, lizards, —
> Here's bright Everlasting!
> Here's a crumb of Forever!
> Here's a crumb of Forever!

I have said that Miss Bogan has a sharp sense of objects, the eye that can pluck out from the welter of experience the inevitable image. And she loves the words, the nouns particularly, rich in human association. "Baroque Comment" ends:

> Crown and vesture; palm and laurel chosen as noble and enduring;
> Speech proud in sound; death considered sacrifice;
> Mask, weapon, urn; the ordered strings;
> Fountains; foreheads under weather-bleached hair;
> The wreath, the oar, the tool,
> The prow;
> The turned eyes and the opened mouth of love.

But let us see how this side of her talent operates when she is absolutely open, as in the deeply moving elegy "To My Brother":

O you so long dead,
You masked and obscure,
I can tell you, all things endure:
The wine and the bread;

The marble quarried for the arch;
The iron become steel;
The spoke broken from the wheel;
The sweat of the long march;

The hay-stacks cut through like loaves
And the hundred flowers from the seed;
All things indeed
Though struck by the hooves

Of disaster, of time due,
Of fell loss and gain,
All things remain,
I can tell you, this is true.

Though burned down to stone
Though lost from the eye,
I can tell you, and not lie, —
Save of peace alone.

The imagery in some of the last poems is less specific, yet still strongly elemental; we have, I think, what Johnson called the grandeur of generality. They are timeless, impersonal in a curious way and objective—not highly idiosyncratic as so much of the best American work is. Her poems can be read and reread: they keep yielding new meanings, as all good poetry should. The ground beat of the great tradition can be heard, with the necessary subtle variations. Bogan is one of the true inheritors. Her poems create their own reality, and demand not just attention, but the emotional and spiritual response of the whole man. Such a poet will never be popular, but can and should be a true model for the young. And the best work will stay in the language as long as the language survives.

A Psychic Janitor

Selected notebook entries (1959–63), first
published in *Straw for the Fire*.

AS A CRITIC, I am no more than a janitor, a psychic janitor clean-
ing up what others have left sorting through—could it be some
beautiful poem, or rubbish?

§

I don't care what a writer claims, or what, even, he talks about—
even if the talk is good—that's for the discursive, albeit organized
mind, for academia, for the lecturer, for the logic-choppers, the
whereto and why boys. This is all second-order creation of
reality. Poetry is, first, last, and foremost creation, the supreme
creation, for me, at least in language… I'm sick of fumbling,
furtive, disorganized minds like bad lawyers trying to make too
many points that *this* is an age of criticism: and these, mind you,
tin-eared punks who couldn't tell a poem from an old boot if a
gun were put to their heads. These jerks who know twelve lines
of Dante, the early Tiresome Tom, and Ezra Pound's laundry
notes. These are the most monstrous, most pretentious arbiters
that yet appeared on the academic scene.

§

There's another typical stance: only *I* hear it. Then just listen:
hump, schlump, bump—half the time: a real—did I say real?—
I mean *unreal,* unnatural—thumping away in stupid staves, an
arbitrary lopping of lines, rhythms, areas of experience, a turning
away from much of life, an exalting of a few limited areas of human
consciousness. All right, I say, make like that, and die in your own
way: in other words limited, provincial, classical in a distorted and

—I use the word carefully—degraded sense; "American" in the sense American means eccentric, warped, and confined.

I am fed up with some of the poems of self-congratulation by our poetic elders, that *I have lived a life of self-control* sort of thing, that gruesome spiritual smugness that comes from being ever so talky with and about God—God, Job, and the Lord Jesus himself. There's no doubt, once we are aware of, once we venture into the area of the spiritual all dangers increase—there's always spiritual pride, that greatest of sins...

There's more than one variety of disease in this area of experience: the tiny epiphany, the cozy moment in the suburban rose garden, the ever so slight shimmer in the face of afternoon reality —not much more than the Georgians seemed to be talking about...

§

A lot of tired beetles, these American classicists. It's as if the effort to be austere has left them with nothing much else than the impulse to congratulate themselves on being something else than their contemporaries—small-fry Hemingways who have read Homer.

§

I'm aware that among the expert (unfrightened) trans-Atlantic literary theologians to approach God without benefit of clergy is a grievous lapse in taste, if not a mortal sin. But in crawling out of a swamp, or up what small rock-faces I try to essay, I don't need a system on my back.

§

TWO RETORTS TO ELIOT

I.

Our God Himself adores
Only *beasts* upon all fours:
Humility's for bores.

II.

What do we need to foil intolerable Fate?
A God we kiss to, standing on our feet.

§

Essay: I Hate Eliot

1ST sentence. Why?

Because I love him too much—

§

The pseudo-poem; the whipped-up poem; the "decoration," the intimacies of bogus and shoddy love affairs; the insights acquired running between the boudoir and the altar; rewritten St. Theresa and St. Catherine.

§

What poetry may need at this point is a *certain* vulgarity, not *all* vulgarities. What Synge referred to: the brutality, in a word, the aliveness of life.

§

What's *important?* That which is dug out of books, or out of the guts? What's important? Lacerations, whipped-up accusations, interlarded schoolboy Latin quotations, or the language really modified, a new rhythm... ?

§

If we muddle and thump through a paraphrase, with side comments, however brilliant, we still do not have the poem.

§

For the poem—even the fairly good poem—means an entity, a unity has been achieved that transcends by far the organization of the lecture, the essay, even the great speech. This the academics at least should know—and more and more of them do. They were put on the world to understand this: it's high time some of them did.

§

We cry against the critics: because it's so important they be better.

§

I think poetic experience in the modern world must, of necessity, be primarily concerned with depth rather than breadth. A Goethe is no longer possible; but an intense personal poetry...

§

I've always found Robert Frost's remark about free verse—he'd rather play tennis with the net down—I've always found this wonderfully suggestive, as an old coach, in a great number of ways. For one thing I coached at Penn State. We played in clothing cast off—laundered of course—by the football team. Of course, my derriere being what it is, I frequently found not only the net at least semi-down, but also my pants... You know how things get from too much laundering: the rubber in the various intimate equipment disintegrates, the string would bust in my sweat pants: there'd be a hole in my racket. Well, do you get the analogy: that's me and free verse. Frost, he had a racket and balls all his life; but some of us out in the provinces operated under difficulties: we've had our disorganized lives and consequently our intractable material: we've had to use free verse, on occasion.

§

I never could understand the objection to "free" verse—it's only bad, i.e. slack, lax, sloppy free verse one objects to. For the net, in final terms, is stretched even tighter. Since the poet has neither stanza form nor rhyme to rely on, he has to be more cunning than ever, in manipulating, modulating his sounds, and keeping that forward propulsion, and making it all natural. Instead of end-rhyme, of course, he has internal rhyme, assonance, consonance. But he can't fall back on tradition as much as a formalist. It's the pause, the natural pause that matters, Lawrence said somewhere —said it better, of course. He has to depend more on his own ear.

We seem to be shyer of the prose-poem than the French. Maybe it fits their language better... I rather think this: that the modern poet can afford to get closer to prose much more easily and profitably and less dangerously than the writer of prose can afford to be "poetic." I think of how spongy, how ersatz some of those passages from Virginia Woolf are...

Let's say it's another kind of thing, maybe a lesser thing, the settable song, but let's also admit that it is enormously difficult to do. After all there was Shakespeare, and Campion, and even the Joyce of *Chamber Music*. And there are those who think Yeats's plays were mere settings to the songs within them... It depends on the very energy of the psyche, the inner ear. The Victorians, many of them, were tired, and they wrote a tired poetry, though often subtle rhythmically. *"I am half-sick of shadows," said the Lady of Shalott*. She didn't have the spiritual guts to peer into the black, to take a full look at the worst.

It became a whole psychological stance which Yeats himself picks up in his youth: the tired young man on the sofa; today we have the tired young man in the gutter.

Understand I'm not making a cult of violent energy in itself. One is often offended, for instance, by Browning's huffing and puffing, let's-have-no-nonsense sort of thing; and some of the bouncy ballads of Chesterton and the other English balladists I can't abide; or the heavy swats that Housman sometimes will use in his ballad metres. But let's hasten to say that Housman can modulate beautifully...

As our poetry has become increasingly dramatic, in the sense it often represents a struggle or a dialogue between our selves (didn't Yeats say we make of our quarrels with others, rhetoric; of our quarrels with ourselves, poetry?): and with these poems becoming longer, often representing the protagonist under considerable stress, poets have had to learn to write a poetry that follows the motion of the mind itself: hence some of the associational jumps, the shifts, in subject matter and rhythm, the changes in speed. That is, the poet does not merely talk, or ruminate, he cries out in turn, in agony, in rage. This puts enormous demands on the writer: it is as if he is writing the high scenes in a tragic drama. And his shifts, his jumps, his changes of pace have to be imaginatively right, or all is lost; it will be a nothing, a windy bombast. We seem to demand or want a poetry with the personality under great stress.

§

The human mind, in the desperate effort to be gay, has produced so little *real* nonsense, so few funny poems, so few poems of joy.

§

R.F., W.C.W.
The Muse taught them a way of being plain,
Who, like the sun, grew greater going down.

§

In Muir, I find an almost intolerable sense of the sadness of existence.

§

Wilbur: can look at a thing, and talk about it beautifully, can turn it over in his mind, and draw truths from a scene, easily and effortlessly (it would seem)—though his kind of writing requires the hardest kind of discipline, it must be remembered. Not a graceful mind—that's a mistake—but a mind of grace, an altogether different and higher thing.

§

Let the uncharitable, the obtuse say all they will, bringing their charges—sentimentality; of using words (*flowers*) as counters; of creating ambiguous non-states of being; of sniggering; of posturing... ethical self-indulgence; of failing to change after the first two books... of arbitrary syntactical nuttiness;—yet Cummings always remains a throwback if you will, but a throwback to something truly wonderful, almost lost from the language: the secret of being lyrically funny, the secret of being truly alive and happy. He has revived, renewed more than we know. All right, he's father-haunted. Who isn't? He'd be a monster if he were otherwise...

I think of Cummings, not as a poet of one kind of thing, one genre, one singularity, but as one who has explored various and important and often neglected sides of modern sensibility:

1. The child's. Here, it seems to me, he moves within the mind of the child, *is* the child, if you will—without condescending or being coy—an enormously difficult feat.

2. The adolescent's. And this area of experience is a real trap, with the reader so often conditioned by the notion that the young don't really suffer. They're just oversize children with stock reactions, living out the misadventures of inexperience, uttering only stylized lingo, boring as advertising formulae.

There are these randy various jumpings, a many-faceted marvelous man.

He is not content to doodle along in the five-foot line.

In an age of cozy-toe operators, he has always been ready to take a chance…

§

Put it this way: I detest dogs, but adore wolves.

§

I'm beginning to think like a novelist. Is that death?

§

How crude, how irrelevant those reports of reality called fiction! The worst honest poems are better. Who cares that Arnold Bennett ever lived? Or even Huxley?

§

Fitzgerald: He was born, and died, a Princeton sophomore. (A Princeton sophomore was cute; we, at least, were sinister. We didn't play at being gangsters, we were gangsters.)

§

If I could but respect prose! — would I be happy?

§

In poetry, there are no casual readers.

§

My hope younger than I, of course,
Disdains Yeatsian remorse;
That balm of academic wits,

And sophomoric sugar-tits.
Remorse for what?

§

The imagist poet: runs out of objects, his eye tires.

§

Perhaps the poet's path is closer to the mystic than we think: his thought becomes more imageless.

§

The body of imagery, possibly, thins out or purifies itself or the mind moves into a more abstract mode, closer to wisdom, in talent of a high order.

§

Those without poetry: their source of innocence lost.

§

"But reading poetry is as natural an activity as eating one's breakfast." Alas, some people associate it with other natural functions.

§

People can and do understand poetry but they don't want to: it is a danger.

§

O Muse, when shall I arrive at a true sense of history,
I who have served pre-history so long and well?

§

An eager young coed was poised with her pencil. What is the most interesting phenomenon in American poetry, Mr. Roethke? What I do next, he said, abandoning her for a ham sandwich. My

Gaad, he's rude, she said. No, he's just hungry. His tapeworm just had a nervous breakdown.

§

Anonymous is my favorite author.

Epilogue

A Tirade Turning

Published posthumously under the pseudonym
Winterset Rothberg in *Encounter* (December 1963).

I THINK OF MY MORE TEDIOUS CONTEMPORARIES:

Roaring asses, hysterics, sweet-myself beatniks, earless wonders
happy with effects a child of two could improve on: verbal delin-
quents; sniggering, mildly obscene souser-wowsers, this one writing
as if only he had a penis, that one bleeding, but always in waltz-
time; another intoning, over and over, in metres the expert have
made hideous; the doleful, almost-good, overtrained technicians—
what a mincing explicitness, what a profusion of adjectives, what a
creaking of adverbs!

—And those life-hating hacks, the critics without sensibility,
masters of a castrated prose, readers of one book by any given au-
thor (or excerpts thereof), aware of one kind of effect, lazy dishon-
est arrogant generalizers, tasteless anthologists, their lists of merit,
their values changing with every whim and wind of academic fash-
ion; wimble-wamble essayists; philosophers without premise; bony
bluestocking commentators, full of bogus learning; horse-faced
lady novelists, mere slop-jars of sensibility

—And those rude provincial American classicists, thumping
along in a few clumsy staves, congratulating themselves in every
other poem on their spiritual fortitude, their historical perspicacity,
their ineffable god-like integrity; only-I-hear-it miniature Yvors,
their sound effects usually the harsh rasp of a cracked kazoo; grace-
ful anachronisms, trapped in one wavering collective image; again
maundering Wordsworthians, becalmed in dear William's Sky
Canoe, throbbing back into the caves of cold dismay; timid Cole-
ridges, swallowing Seconal, sucking at greasy reefers or dead cigars;

undelightful bowerbirds wafting their faint quavers to enraptured sophomores; peripheral twitterers, their toes turned upward

—Two-dimensional dreamers: barnyard mystics, braying for eternity; Jesus-creeping somnambulist converts, clutching their rosaries, slobbering over fake Arab bones, unaware of anyone else, living or dead

—The duchess of could-you, would-you, with her acrid asides and her lady's maid diction. (When I think of her, God thickens my tongue.)

—The professionally sincere; slug-nutty nihilists; misty-moisty mush-mouthed muttonheads; Arthur Saltonstall Robinson Flubb, iv; Henry Mortimer Clift, v; Miniver Cheevy Minsky, composer of salutes to space needles and astronauts; whistling ogres; metaphysical wailers; purveyors of tired literary ham-and-cheese, gefülte fish, dead bananas; crazy rhapsodical lady poets running between religious retreats and national bridge tournaments; suburban Sapphos, decked out like female impersonators, leaning over the podium, dugs a-droop, moaning, barking like sea-lionesses

—And that breathless bounding moon-faced bourgeois bully-for-you boy, beaming idiotic goodwill from every oily pore, blowing and billowing silly bromides, belching baked beans, inane homilies, inept praises, fake epiphanies, reveling in gracelessness, obtuse awkwardness, all wrong about everything that matters, mutters, or farts in a parcel

—And the professionally insane, stepping in and out of the madhouse as others would out of their baths, happy with their half-literate therapists, condemned out of their own mouths, self-indulgent, uncharitable, insentient.

—And what of the Dylan-adorers, white-eared, fawn-eyed, fervent? Or the two-bit cisatlantic tough guys making like Marlon Brando on a motor scooter, Edna St. Vincent Millay on a raft, Rupert Brooke in a balloon, Robert P. Tristram Coffin on a blueberry muffin?

O bottom hot-cake, O hesitant pretzel,
O mile-high meringue, O prodigious pudding,
O caperer in the Kangaroo Room,

O poet of the fireplug, the privet-hedge, the second floor, the
        back porch, the decayed brothel, the English Institute,
—O maimed waif of change!—
Was it reading you I first felt, full in my face, the hot blast of
        clatter of insane machinery?
Yet heard,
Beneath the obscene murderous noises of matter gone mad,
Whose grinding dissonance threatens to overwhelm us all,
The small cry of the human?

I, the loneliest semi-wretch alive, a stricken minor soul,
Weep to you now;
But I've an eye to your leaping forth and your fresh ways of
        wonder;
And I see myself beating back and forth like stale water in a
        battered pail;
Are not you my final friends, the fair cousins I loathe and love?
That man hammering I adore, though his noise reach the very
        walls of my inner self;
Behold, I'm a heart set free, for I have taken my hatred and
        eaten it,
The last acrid sac of my rat-like fury;
I have succumbed, like all fanatics, to my imagined victims;
I embrace what I perceive!
Brothers and sisters, dance ye,
Dance ye all!

The Beautiful Disorder

Selected notebook entries (1954–63) which appeared originally in *Pebble* (1971) before being published in *Straw for the Fire*.

So IT'S TO BEGIN BY BEGINNING, and what words I have won't bring you to love—for the language of this life. It's you I mean, already in a half-drowse of stale fancies, absurd notions of meter, muddy welters of unbeautiful thoughts, the turgid lyrics of adolescence. For it's one of the muddiest times of all—worse than senility, in some ways, for Grandma at least remembers, and has said and thought her dreary little tags so often that they have a finish and a rhythm…

Roaring asses, hysterics, I invoke you. I ask your unquiet aid in this collective dismembering and dissemination of wits…

§

We can't escape what we are, and I'm afraid many of my notions about verse (I haven't too many) have been conditioned by the fact that for nearly twenty-five years I've been trying to teach the young something about the nature of verse by writing it—and that with very little formal knowledge of the subject or previous instruction. So it's going to be like Harpo Marx teaching the harp.

§

My doctor says I have fantasies of omnipotence about teaching: that I can teach any idiot, in the course of three quarters, to write at least one piece of verse that an intelligent man can read with pleasure.

$

Those students get the highest grades who take their responsibilities of educating me most seriously.

$

I have only a few ideas; and some of them are almost dead from overwork...

$

I think at least we have this distinction: the Russians, up to now, haven't claimed to have invented "Creative Writing." Frankly, as far as I'm concerned, they're welcome to it.

$

... In part you accept what "I" know: but I also am most anxious to find out what *you* know, care about, like, listen to, are moved by: no one hears everything; even the greatest can make absurd errors in judgment—particularly with reference to contemporaries. Goethe and Schiller let Hölderlin pass by under their noses, but the really good ones, the intense passionate ones, had their contemporaries sized up: look at Hopkins on Browning, on Wordsworth; think how acute Keats was in sensing the odious pomposity in Wordsworth. The wonder of wonders is the unanimity of judgment among practicing writers...

Before you are wild, you first have to be, not tame, but capable of being contained; or containing yourself, your psyche: that which is stored up.

So, and I admit that to an extent I set myself up as an arbiter, think of me as a spy from outside who has come back with good news...

$

I expect you to be human beings. Don't laugh—that's already an incredible assumption: they're a disappearing species.

$

Remember nestlings: I'm here to see you live.

§

I'm paid to remind you what you are.

§

Poetry-writing (the craft) can't be taught, but it can be insinuated.

§

Not inspiration but the breaking down of strong habitual barriers.

§

There are only a few little secrets. If I give them to you all at once, you would be addled. For each truth has its stage.

§

Make ready for your gifts. Prepare. Prepare.

§

Our problem is to get something done, to get started somewhere, away from the rubbish of our respective corners, out of coma or confusion toward some crack of the light, some piece of what really is.

§

Allow me a certain sententiousness, since this comes from a desire to have you avoid my own mistakes.

§

But let me say what I'm up to.

1st, To point out a few of the elements, structural or otherwise, which seem to make for the memorable, particularly striking lines.

2nd, To show how texture affects rhythm, particularly in the song-like poem.

3rd, To indicate a few of the strategies open to the writer of the irregular prose-like poem.

§

There's one kind of prose-poem which is simply provided by the succession of events. This can be enormously hard to do—and not destroy the emphasis by blowing the material beyond what it is, becoming portentous or just plain dull... The nature of the subject can provide, can be the expediency: when the thing is seen long enough, observed intensely enough, if one is sufficiently involved emotionally, the details dribble out. The poem takes a kind of natural shape.

§

You will live, at times, to curse your sense of form: How much easier it is to sprawl all over, to be a mere receiver...

§

Form acts the father: tells you what you may and may not do.

§

A writer can get trapped in a form, in a psychological stance, an attitude, and he must struggle, often, to extricate himself or he may die...

§

Any form, even those great ones hallowed by tradition, can become a trap.

§

The sonnet: a great form to pick your nose in.

§

A more objective and more oblique art depends less upon the language itself, is less likely to be defiled or worn by time.

§

One does not become another poet by simply adoring him, by making him a psychic pin-up boy.

§

Someone said you have been influenced? Indeed, and no doubt
you also drank your mother's milk.

§

Advice to the young: don't fret too much about being
"influenced," but make sure you chew up your old boy with a
vengeance, blood, guts, and all.

§

For poetry, my dear, is not
Things other people said & thought
        Nor what you're thinking.

§

I want you to rise above Spokane!

§

It's hard work, and you won't want it for long. Never mind being
a mad poet; just concentrate on being a poet, for the time being.
And it's not true, as Freud or some other mythologist has said,
that everyone can write nonsense.

§

Don't try to refine your singularities all at once. Don't work too
hard at being nutty—you may make it all too soon, our culture
being what it is.

§

One trouble is of course... that the poet in mid-career, as I may
say, or should it be male menopause—all his masks begin to
disappear or he begins to disappear before all his masks: the
roaring boy, the bully of the campus, the beast of Bennington,
the raping tinker of Chenango Valley.

§

I confess to a certain fondness for these poems: perhaps they
have, like some bastards, the charm of a community effort.

§

A defective rhythmic sense which comes from wrenching language
into a pattern almost a poem (related to prose sensibility). The
management of the syllable is the very core of the problem: I think
it is related to the question of articulation itself: the voice box…

§

Phase 37: That every damn thing one does is a manifestation
of genius.

§

I'm the genius of the world, of that there is no doubt.
Said Epictetus to the foetus, Does your mother know you're out?

§

The young poet feels in himself powers which are far from being
expressed: he wishes to be honored for his impulse, not the
performance.

§

The greatest assassin of life is haste.

§

There can be not-work of great emotional charge: necessary to
the growth of the soul and to one's technical advancement (Are
they so different?).

§

There is a point in the slow progress to maturity when thinking
about oneself becomes no longer a major pleasure…

§

Leave "truths" to your elders, and take on the burden of observation.

§

Nothing seen, nothing said.

§

Not only to perceive the single thing sharply: but to perceive the relationships between many things sharply perceived.

§

A figure is a judgment, so they say;
The mind can never take a holiday:
It's not the pure irrational we know:
The forebrain likes its children to be slow.

§

I think we could do with more style, more assonance, more élan, more verve, more animal spirits, more *fun*. These are not solemn matters.

§

The comic—the really funny before the eye of God—is harder to achieve than the lyric; more anguishing, more exacting, more exhausting to its writer.

§

Variation: there's a technical problem: when to rest. But it need not bother you who rest so easy.

§

Rare the writer who knows what his material really is, particularly the young writer.

§

The point comes when any honest writer will come to realize he is done with a particular body of material: that henceforward everything in that vein may be eminently respectable, perhaps even better than anyone else could do—but none the less a little less good, the edge not quite so sharp, and this point should be recognized early.

§

Bring to poetry the passion that goes into politics or buying a piece of meat.

§

I recommend that you go, on your own, and immediately, to poets closer to your own age. Some may reflect your own confusions—let them be nameless—read *them* passionately *and* critically.

§

To enter the mind of his contemporaries—that surely is one of the tasks of the artist.

§

I don't say, Come off it: I say stay with it, come on it, do it *grosser* and greater, larger and fatter, earlier and later.

§

Energy is the soul of poetry. Explosive active language.

§

Artist's problem: to get to the best in one's self. And then get away from it.

§

The difficulty comes, at times, from the loss of perspective. There's no great harm in being somebody else once in a while.

There you will come to know how, by working slowly, to be spontaneous.

To bring the poem to what it should be and more.

Such interior meltings, sighs, outcries of ravishment, rose-blown, fly-blown fantasies.

Yet some thefts are reprehensible; this is what is worrying you...

§

The crimes: wasting technical skill on a trivial theme; being idiotically addicted to form, stanza form; doodling with dead diction.

§

There's a point where plainness is no longer a virtue, when it becomes excessively bald, wrenched.

§

The literal—that grave of all the dull.

§

It's the shifting of the thought that's important, often—the rightness (or wrongness!) of the imaginative jump. Many modern poets still are content only with the logical progression, or with metaphors—often beautiful, elaborate, fresh—but these consisting of little more than a listing of appositives. In the richest poetry even the juxtaposition of objects should be pleasurable; hence, Neruda, even in indifferent translation, is pleasurable.

§

To make the line in itself interesting, syntactically, that is the problem.

§

A paradox: more know what a poem is than what a line is...

§

A many-sided man has many rhythms.

§

We have forgotten the importance of the list. We have the better surrealists to remind us.

§

All great breaks in consciousness or styles are very simple; but enormously important.

§

It is the mark of the true poet that he perpetually renews himself.

§

"I've learned a lot in this course. I don't understand a thing you say, but I just watch your hands." Hardly a tribute to one's verbal powers.

§

I had eaten the apple ere you were weaned. I bring the derision of walls, enchantress sure of your body, extremest oriole. What little you have shown me, I love—like my own first fat-fingered effusion...

§

I don't care if you crawled on your knees from Timbuctoo: and think me the greatest thing since the living Buddha: I'll not, no I'll not nurse you, etc. Every poet must be, has to be, remembah: his *own* mother...

§

The poem, even a short time after being written, seems no miracle; unwritten, it seems something beyond the capacity of the gods.

§

The thing conceived; the thing finally said—a vast distance.

§

Every sentence a cast into the dark.

§

What is hard to endure—the peculiar and haunting sense that
one is about to write a poem, and then have no poem come; or be
interrupted by trivia, by fools, by sense.

§

You must believe: a poem is a holy thing—a good poem, that is.

§

Remind yourself once more of the absolute holiness of your task.

§

To write poetry: you have to be prepared to die.

§

A schoolmaster should *not* like to keep his disciples.

§

Create: then disown.

§

You've led me to more than I am.
O lead me on, brief children,
To those white regions where no soul is spoiled.

§

I am overwhelmed by the beautiful disorder of poetry, the eternal
virginity of words.

Appendix

Appendix

Introduction to *On the Poet and His Craft* (1965)

AMONG THE IMPORTANT POETS of our century few have avoided altogether the writing of essays or lectures, critical prose. For some —T.S. Eliot and Ezra Pound spring immediately to mind as perhaps the most obvious examples—the efforts in prose were calculated to clear the ground for their poetry: a necessary maneuver because that poetry was new and experimental, radical in conception and execution, and it required the education of a taste by which it could be appreciated. The case of William Butler Yeats is something else again. We find the entire, wide range of his interests—in Irish folklore, politics, and the theater; in mysticism and the occult; in poetry and symbolism; in his own life, the friends, circumstances, and preoccupations which shaped it—taking its full share in the production of his prose. On the other hand, the prose of Wallace Stevens seems simply an extension of the thought, the metaphysical enterprise informing his poetry but stripped of the poetry's linguistic elegance and metaphorical richness, though often compensating for this with an aphoristic precision.

The prose writings which Theodore Roethke left behind him at his death in August 1963 hardly differ from those of the other poets I have mentioned in consisting almost exclusively of occasional pieces: book reviews, prefaces and introductions, broadcasts, university lectures, statements about his own work or autobiographical remarks for a reference book, parodies and satires. Roethke was not, however, nor is it likely that he would have become had he lived another twenty-five or thirty years, a poet who was also a critical theorist, who proposed some new departure from existing poetic forms in which all writers should participate or who announced a moment that would revolutionize literature. Yet he was, as even the lightest perusal of his poems will amply demonstrate, a writer who, in the practical sphere, carried out—and how beautifully and successfully too!—some of the most astonishing experiments in the history of modern verse. At the same time, he maintained, as the other side of his poetic endeavor, a commitment to the traditional lyric as it has been practiced from the Elizabethans to Yeats, and on to Stanley Kunitz and Louise Bogan. While Roethke's prose sets forth neither programs nor theories, it does provide, again and again, in explanations of purpose with regard to his own work, and in discussion and judgment of the work of others, his fundamental aims and his beliefs about the art of poetry. Though his prose pieces are miscellaneous, not usually ordered to any end beyond the subject at hand, and sometimes repeat one another slightly, they have the advantage of being perhaps truer and of greater authenticity because they lack the self-consciousness or the rhetorical motives which often mar more theoretical statements.

Roethke's prose, from the early reviews of Mark Van Doren, Spanish loyalist poets, and others, to his later and more personal pieces such as "Open Letter" or "Some Remarks on Rhythm," is always instantaneously recognizable as that of a working poet who takes his vocation very seriously indeed. The identifying mark in this respect is, I believe, a constant, unflagging attention to matters of craft and form, the fundamentals of the poem on which everything else is built and depends. And when he is not discussing such details with reference to Ben Belitt or Louise Bogan, he is doing so in writing about literary influences on his own poetry ("How to Write like Somebody Else") or in treating some of the many problems which confront the teacher of poetry ("A Word to the Instructor") and the poet-teacher who conducts a workshop course in the composition of verse ("The Teaching Poet"). Again, Roethke's concern with these affairs is not theoretical or purely speculative; he was as concretely aware as any poet could be of the forces molding his work, stirring his imagination; and he was a teacher of many years' experience, as well as of legendary reputation. For him, the making of a poem by an individual, a student, the honesty, tenacity, labor of craftsmanship it demanded, in addition to the gifts donated by the imagination, comprised a unique and worthy human act;

whether the poem which resulted from it was a masterpiece or only a minor success was unimportant in comparison with what was attempted. We might point out here that a continuation of this attitude characterizes Roethke's valuations of other poets: he took little interest in literary fashion or critical reputation in estimating poetry; writers are not judged by their names, their innovations, their place in some invented hierarchy, but specifically, with the performance of each isolated poem.

In a number of essays and lectures, several heretofore unpublished, Roethke openly discusses his own poetry and portions of the background of experience from which it derived. When his many notebooks are edited and published, as they undoubtedly will be in the coming years, we shall learn much more about the development of this magnificent poet, and learn it in detail at the source. But for the purposes of his readers now, there is a good deal to be discovered and gained from attention to pieces like "Open Letter," in which the sequence poems of childhood from *The Lost Son* and *Praise to the End!* are commented upon at length; "Some Remarks on Rhythm," which not only offers excellent statements about sound and rhythm in poetry but also points, in certain of its remarks, to the technique of the long, free lines, the "catalogue" use of descriptive detail, so prominent in the "North American Sequence" from *The Far Field*; and "An American Poet Introduces Himself and His Poems" and "On 'Identity,'" both of which supply interesting biographical material, indicate something of this poet's direction and his convictions. No one who has found Roethke's poetry to be rich and moving will, I believe, be disappointed by his prose. Once we have understood that the pieces included here were written for definite occasions, and that Roethke was not otherwise much given to expressing himself publicly in prose but devoted himself wholeheartedly to his poems, then we shall know how to approach them. Even his book reviews contain sharp, valuable observations, and we should be the poorer for not having them readily available. It is my hope that this small collection of Theodore Roethke's prose will stand on book shelves along with the volumes of his poetry, for these essays, lectures, and reviews are worth turning to repeatedly for the help they give us, deepening our insight into the work and adding to our minds from this fine poet's store of wisdom about poetic art.

I have divided this book into four sections. The first, which begins with a paper Roethke wrote as a student at the University of Michigan, includes several statements about his life and work. Section two is composed of various papers on the craft of poetry—on his own poems, aspects of poetry in general, and comments about the teaching of verse. Two memoirs, one of Dylan Thomas, plus two extravagant prose pieces written under the pseudonym "Winterset Rothberg" make up a third part. Finally, in section four, I have placed most of Roethke's book reviews, as well as an introduction to a selection of poems by several contemporary poets and his full-length essay on Louise Bogan, whose work—like that of Léonie Adams, Stanley Kunitz, and Rolfe Humphries, among others—he so strongly admired. A late "Winterset Rothberg" piece, posthumously published, appears as an epilogue.

I should like to offer here my warmest thanks to Beatrice Roethke, the poet's widow, for her initial suggestion that I edit this collection, and for her unfailing help and kindness. Miss Judith Johnson of the Manuscripts Section of the University of Washington library has aided me in many ways with information about papers and in handling matters of permissions. Mr. John W. Matheson's bibliography of Roethke has been of invaluable help in locating and identifying material. I should like to thank as well Mrs. Irving Gold for her typing of the manuscript of this book, and Mr. Maurice English for suggesting its title.

Ralph J. Mills Jr.
University of Chicago, 1965

About the Author

THEODORE ROETHKE WAS BORN in Saginaw, Michigan, in 1908. As a child, he spent much time in the greenhouse owned by his father and uncle. His impressions of the natural world contained there would later profoundly influence the subjects and imagery of his verse. Roethke attended the University of Michigan and took a few classes at Harvard, but was unhappy in school. His first book, *Open House* (1941), took ten years to write and was critically acclaimed upon its publication. He went on to publish sparingly, but his reputation grew with each new collection, including *The Waking* which was awarded the Pulitzer Prize in 1954.

He admired the writing of such poets as Emerson, Thoreau, Whitman, Blake, and Wordsworth, as well as Yeats and Dylan Thomas. Roethke had close literary friendships with fellow poets W.H. Auden, Louise Bogan, Stanley Kunitz, and William Carlos Williams. He taught at various colleges and universities, including Lafayette, Pennsylvania State, and Bennington, and worked last at the University of Washington, where he was mentor to a generation of Northwest poets that included David Wagoner, Carolyn Kizer, and Richard Hugo. Theodore Roethke died in 1963.

LANNAN LITERARY SELECTIONS 2001

Hayden Carruth, *Doctor Jazz*

Norman Dubie, *The Mercy Seat:
Collected & New Poems, 1967–2001*

Theodore Roethke, *On Poetry & Craft*

Ann Stanford, *Holding Our Own:
The Selected Poems of Ann Stanford*

Mónica de la Torre & Michael Wiegers, editors,
Reversible Monuments: Contemporary Mexican Poetry

For more on the Lannan Literary Selections,
visit our web site:

www.coppercanyonpress.org

The Chinese character for poetry is made up of two parts: "word" and "temple."
It also serves as pressmark for Copper Canyon Press.

Founded in 1972, Copper Canyon Press remains dedicated to publishing
poetry exclusively, from Nobel laureates to new and emerging authors.
The press thrives with the generous patronage of readers, writers, booksellers,
librarians, teachers, students, and funders — everyone who shares the
conviction that poetry invigorates the language and sharpens
our appreciation of the world.

PUBLISHER'S CIRCLE

Allen Foundation for the Arts
Elliott Bay Book Company
Mimi Gardner Gates
Jaech Family Fund
Lannan Foundation
Rhoady and Jeanne Marie Lee
Lila Wallace–Reader's Digest Fund
National Endowment for the Arts
Port Townsend Paper Company
U.S.–Mexico Fund for Culture
Emily Warn and Daj Oberg
Washington State Arts Commission
The Witter Bynner Foundation
Charles and Barbara Wright

For information and catalogs:
COPPER CANYON PRESS
Post Office Box 271
Port Townsend, Washington 98368
360/385-4925
poetry@coppercanyonpress.org
www.coppercanyonpress.org

The typefaces used in this book come to us from the Dutch Baroque. Janson Text is derived from the designs of Hungarian traveling scholar Nicholas Kis while he worked in Anton Janson's Amsterdam workshop in the 1680s. The titles are set in Berthold Van Dijck Titling, based on the work of Christoffel van Dijck, from the 1660s. Book design and composition by Valerie Brewster, Scribe Typography. Printed on archival-quality Glatfelter Author's Text at McNaughton & Gunn, Inc.

§